QUICK WIN B2B SALES

Answers to your top 100 B2B sales questions

Ray Collis & John O'Gorman

Published by
OAK TREE PRESS
19 Rutland Street, Cork, Ireland
www.oaktreepress.com

A catalogue record of this book is
available from the British Library.

ISBN 978 1 904887 48 5

INTRODUCTION

QUICK WIN B2B SALES is aimed at sales professionals who are interested in new ways of boosting their sales success. It contains the answers to the questions most commonly asked by sales people selling business-to-business solutions – questions that relate to the principal sales opportunities and challenges faced everyday.

You can read **QUICK WIN B2B SALES** cover-to-cover, or you can dip in and out of it to find the answer a specific question. Either way, you will find the questions and answers:

- Are practical and to the point.
- Provide tips and techniques that can be put immediately into effect.
- Can be applied in respect of sales valued at €1,000 or €100,000.
- Focus not just on winning a once-off sale, but on building profitable customer relationships.
- Adopt a scientific approach to selling, emphasising the importance of continuous improvement and ongoing learning.

QUICK WIN B2B SALES groups the key sales questions according to the stage of the sales process to which they apply, recognising that there are many dimensions to the B2B sales role, and many steps through which the sale must progress. Thus, there are seven sections to the book:

- **Sales Essentials** sets the scene and answers some of the most common questions about selling.
- **Sales Leads** deals with how to generate more, and better, leads and enquires.

- **Sales Meetings** deals with how to make meetings with prospects more effective, especially the first tentative encounter.
- **Sales Cycles** addresses how buyer and seller can engage more successfully in matching needs to solutions.
- **Sales Orders** focuses on increasing win rates through more effective sales proposals, closing and negotiation.
- **Repeat Sales** focuses on how to generate more revenue from existing customers through more effective account management, project / delivery management and referrals.
- **Sales Management** focuses on issues of concern to sales managers, such as sales systems, the sales team and the sales plan.

In addition, using the grid in the **Contents**, you can search for questions and answers across a range of topics, including:

- Message & Materials.
- Skills.
- Strategy.
- Systems & Structures.

And, where appropriate, answers cross-reference to other questions for a fuller explanation or more information.

Enjoy the book – we wish you lots of quick wins and success in your B2B sales!

Ray Collis & John O'Gorman
Dublin
September 2010

CONTENTS

Search by theme:

Or search by topic:

- Message & Materials.
- Skills.
- Strategy.
- Systems & Structures.

  using the grid overleaf.

SALES ESSENTIALS	Message & Materials	Skills	Strategy	Systems & Structures	PAGE
Q1 How is B2B selling different?		☑	☑		2
Q2 Why is it important to take a long-term view in sales?			☑		5
Q3 How can we align sales and marketing?			☑		7
Q4 How can we drive our sales and marketing?			☑	☑	9
Q5 What do we need to know before we launch a new product / service?		☑	☑		11
Q6 How do we start selling in international markets?	☑	☑	☑		13
Q7 Is there a better way to forecast sales than relying on market research?	☑	☑	☑		15

SALES LEADS	Message & Materials	Skills	Strategy	Systems & Structures	PAGE
Q8 What trends are changing the way sales messages are heard?			☑		18
Q9 Why is strategic focus so important?			☑		20
Q10 How do we define the profile of our ideal target customer?			☑		22
Q11 How do we generate demand?	☑		☑		24
Q12 What are the 10 key steps in generating demand?	☑		☑		25

SALES MEETINGS	Message & Materials	Skills	Strategy	Systems & Structures	PAGE
Q24 Should we be honest with the customer – always?	☑				49
Q25 What's the difference between 'leads' and 'contacts'?				☑	50
Q26 Why should we 'stop selling'?			☑	☑	52
Q27 What is it buyers want to hear?	☑				54
Q28 What can I do to make sales meetings more effective?	☑			☑	55
Q29 How do we position ourselves as experts?			☑	☑	58
Q30 What questions can we ask to help identify buyers' needs?	☑				60
Q31 What questions should we ask in an early-stage meeting with a buyer?	☑				62
Q32 What should we do to make sure of a great sales presentation?	☑			☑	64
Q33 What follow-up should we do after a sales meeting?				☑	65

SALES CYCLES	Message & Materials	Skills	Strategy	Systems & Structures	PAGE
Q34 What is the sales cycle?				☑	68
Q35 How do I know whether a prospect represents a genuine sales opportunity?			☑	☑	69

SALES CYCLES	Message & Materials	Skills	Strategy	Systems & Structures	PAGE
Q36 How can we get the prospect to do our pre-qualification for us?			☑	☑	71
Q37 What are the implications of the client's cost of the buying process to me as a seller?			☑	☑	74
Q38 What questions should we be asking buyers at different stages in the sales cycle?	☑				76
Q39 'To speed up the sale, you must slow down'. What does this mean?	☑		☑	☑	78
Q40 What must we do to win the sale?	☑			☑	80
Q41 How can we help the buyer to buy?	☑			☑	82
Q42 What mistakes will buyers not forgive?	☑			☑	83
Q43 How does a seller's view of a solution differ from the buyer's view?			☑		84
Q44 How can we shorten the sales cycle and accelerate the sale?				☑	86
Q45 How can we use problem identification to sell?	☑				87
Q46 How do we find out what buyers really want?	☑			☑	89
Q47 How do we establish the customer's buying criteria?				☑	91
Q48 What if the buying criteria set are not favourable to our company?	☑			☑	93
Q49 How do we get a good understanding of what motivates the buying organisation and its key people?			☑	☑	95
Q50 How can we change our language / approach to meet buyers' needs better?	☑				97

SALES CYCLES	Message & Materials	Skills	Strategy	Systems & Structures	PAGE
Q51 How can we win over buyers in a downturn?	☑				99
Q52 Does one-to-one selling work?				☑	101
Q53 What is relationship selling?				☑	103
Q54 How can we fast-track our company's credibility for sales purposes?	☑				105
Q55 What rules apply to access to decision-makers in the buying process?				☑	106
Q56 What should the business case look like?	☑				108
Q57 How do we differentiate ourselves from other suppliers?	☑				109
Q58 How do we manage the issue of risk for a buyer?	☑		☑	☑	110
Q59 Why is selling to C-level executives different?	☑		☑	☑	111

SALES ORDERS	Message & Materials	Skills	Strategy	Systems & Structures	PAGE
Q60 How do we price our products / services?			☑		114
Q61 Why should we give our prospects 'homework'?	☑			☑	116
Q62 When should we walk away from a possible sale?			☑	☑	118

SALES ORDERS	Message & Materials	Skills	Strategy	Systems & Structures	PAGE
Q63 How can we make sure our sales proposal is focused on the buyer's needs?	☑				120
Q64 How do we manage a competitive bid?				☑	121
Q65 How can we boost win rates?	☑			☑	123
Q66 How can we improve the hit rate of our proposals?	☑				124
Q67 How should we rate sales opportunities?				☑	125
Q68 How do we spot opportunities that may be in trouble?				☑	127
Q69 'Buyers only buy from big vendors'. What hope have we of selling to them?	☑		☑		129
Q70 How do we know if the sale is ready to close?				☑	131
Q71 What are the most effective closing techniques?	☑	☑			132
Q72 How can we increase our closing success?	☑			☑	134
Q73 What should we do when we lose a sale?				☑	136
Q74 What do we do when a client wants to re-negotiate on price?	☑			☑	138

REPEAT SALES

	Message & Materials	Skills	Strategy	Systems & Structures	PAGE
Q75 Why are pilots risky for sellers?				☑	144
Q76 Why are customers lost?			☑		146
Q77 How can we maximise customer referrals?	☑			☑	147
Q78 We have won the order. The selling is over, right?	☑			☑	150
Q79 What are the main barriers to repeat sales?	☑		☑	☑	152
Q80 Does the salesperson need to be involved after the sale has been won?				☑	153
Q81 How do we increase our importance to the customer?	☑			☑	154
Q82 How do we communicate our importance to the customer?	☑				156
Q83 How do we ensure customer loyalty?			☑		157
Q84 How do we become more pro-active in managing customer relationships?	☑			☑	158
Q85 What are the key elements of account management?				☑	160
Q86 What is the difference between account management and account development?			☑	☑	161
Q87 How can we protect our customers from hungry competitors?	☑			☑	162
Q88 How should we measure customer satisfaction?				☑	164
Q89 Why are referrals so important?			☑		165

SALES MANAGEMENT	Message & Materials	Skills	Strategy	Systems & Structures	PAGE
Q90 Who do we need on our selling team?		☑	☑		168
Q91 What are the obstacles that prevent individual salespeople selling more?				☑	169
Q92 How can we be better at sales forecasting?		☑		☑	171
Q93 Why do we need a sales system?			☑	☑	173
Q94 How do we know our sales system is working properly?				☑	176
Q95 How do we make our sales system more effective?				☑	180
Q96 How can we measure user skills on our sales system?		☑		☑	183
Q97 What can we do when sales staff won't use our sales system?		☑		☑	186
Q98 How can we improve our recruitment of sales staff?		☑		☑	189
Q99 What should our sales plan look like?				☑	190
Q100 How can we increase the effectiveness of our sales team?		☑		☑	192

SALES
ESSENTIALS

Q1   How is B2B selling different?

B2B selling is different. That sounds like a statement of the obvious, yet we meet salespeople everyday whose actions suggest it is not so. They act like the stereotypical salesperson selling double-glazing door-to-door –and then wonder at their lack of success.

B2B selling is about:

- Helping, not selling: Nobody wants to be sold to, but people always welcome help in solving their problems, or identifying how best to meet their needs.

- Solving problems, or exploiting opportunities, not selling products, or services: The customer is not buying products or solutions, nor are they buying just because he / she likes the company or the salesperson. They are buying to solve a problem, or exploit an opportunity within his / her business. The more the salesperson can help him / her do this, the better.

- Listening, not talking: Forgetting this is the most common mistake made by salespeople. They don't shut up long enough for the customer to tell them how they can be helped and convinced to buy the salesperson's product, or service.

- Confidence on the part of the customer, not the salesperson: The super salesperson focuses on building the customer's confidence that your company will best meet their needs.

- Expertise, not salesmanship: That means the customer regards you as an expert, advisor, or specialist, not just a salesperson. It means you can expertly advise potential customers, from a position of knowledge regarding your products and services, as well as their business and industry.

- Benefits, not features: Despite long lists of features, brochures, ads and sales presentations often lack a compelling sales proposition, that:
    - Appeals on a rational, emotional and political level.

- Is tailored to decision-makers / influencers within the target segment.
- Is distinct from competitors.
- Is supported by evidence.
- Presents a clear cost justification.

- A process, not just a person: There is too much emphasis on the salesperson and not enough on the sales process to match the company's solution to the buyer's needs and buying processes. The process must be a clear, logical and repeatable set of steps that correspond to how customers buy; it involves many people in the sales organisation, not just the salesperson.

- Preparation and planning: Time in front of the customer is precious, so great sales people maximise its effectiveness through extensive pre-call research, planning and preparation.

- Opportunities not objections: Great salespeople welcome purchase objections from buyers. They recognise them as opportunities to better understand customer requirements and demonstrate how their solutions can meet them. They deal with them up front and have prepared for and rehearsed how best to answer.

- Enthusiasm! Enthusiasm is a rare, but priceless, quality among salespeople. It is infectious, but cannot be easily mimicked. A sales person has got to believe in the product / service and company he / she is selling.

- Keeping in touch: The one-meeting sale is an illusion, indeed most people you call on may not yet realise they have a problem, or need your solution. By maintaining ongoing contact, you build trust and confidence.

- Long sales cycles: Anything from three to six to 14 months and more. It involves complex buying processes and large buying groups (that is four to six people involved in one way or another in the buying decision). It requires building relationships, credibility and trust, not just demonstrating competitive advantage.

HINT   Help the buyer to solve a problem, or to exploit an opportunity.

See also

Q2   Why is it important to take a long-term view in sales?

Companies that live day-by-day, or quarter-by-quarter, are less successful than those that are capable of looking one, two, or more quarters out. Too many companies live a hand-to-mouth existence, driven by an economic imperative to keep the bills paid. Other may have the funds available, but lack a coherent strategy, the vision and the confidence required to invest in the longer term. Next quarter and next year are a distraction, rather than a focus of attention. For example, most sales managers agree that sending a white paper to a prospect is much more effective than sending a brochure; however, knowing that the former will take time and effort to prepare, they go for the short-term solution and delay the white paper until the next quarter. When next quarter comes, the same thing happens again (and again), and sales results suffer.

A business cannot achieve its long-term objectives by focusing one quarter at a time – for no other reason than that ever-lengthening sales cycles mean that sales and marketing cannot be measured simply in terms of short-term payback.

Here are some reasons why taking a longer term view is vital:

- Generating demand takes time: Exploiting the full potential of prospective customers contacted this quarter – assuming they fit the right profile – requires a sustained effort over several months. Your task is not just to serve existing demand in the marketplace, but to create, or shape, it. It is not enough to focus only on companies actively engaged in a buying decision, or even those with a defined need or budget. Your sales and marketing effort must address the greater number of companies that exhibit longer term potential, but whose needs still may be latent. This requires a long-term investment.

  Maintaining a balanced pipeline involves multiple timelines: Ensuring a balanced pipeline requires action across time horizons, including successfully concluding existing sales cycles / opportunities, this quarter and next; identifying and nurturing opportunities with the potential to generate sales three or four quarters out; and generating fresh leads to go in at the top of the funnel. However, most salespeople admit that they struggle to maintain this balance. In particular, they struggle to balance prospecting with managing opportunities.

- Taking a longer term view is essential to ensuring effectiveness: Too often, marketing and sales initiatives are stand-alone, and not integrated and consistent as the textbooks and intuition tell us they should be. That means one quarter's efforts do not logically reinforce, or complement those of the next. Some prospect companies may be called once and then put aside if not immediately interested, or ready to meet with a salesperson. However, the reality is that the chances of one single contact hitting the right person at the right time – when they are actively pursuing a solution – is small. A longer-term perspective would see these companies being progressively nurtured over time.

- Relationships take time: Just as the one-meeting close is an illusion, so too is the instant relationship, or immediate credibility and trust. After all, a customer cannot trust you until he / she knows you. Building relationships requires an ongoing dialogue and interaction over time. Showing interest and commitment before the sales meeting takes place, as well as after the order is won, is key. In fact, you may win the sale and still be working on the relationship, with repeat sales as the ultimate prize.

See also

Q3 How can we align sales and marketing?

The textbook says 'marketing builds awareness and sales takes advantage of that to sell'. But, with rising sales and marketing costs and finite corporate resources, a fractionalised approach to sales and marketing inevitably retards growth. You need to redefine roles, responsibilities and structures to align sales and marketing more closely. Your marketing should be sales-led, with its activities integrated with sales and focused directly on the pursuit of sales-related objectives.

Here are some tips for aligning sales and marketing:

- Bring sales and marketing together and get communication going. That means meetings, presentations and workshops on both sides, as well as sharing information and staff. Any company committed to effective marketing should expect marketing to spend time in front of customers, going along on sales calls, etc. Of course, this works both ways – salespeople occasionally should sit in on direct marketing campaign meetings, customer focus groups, etc.

- Share information and plans, so that everybody knows what everybody else is doing, what the objectives are and what budget is being spent. Ensure there is formal input, from both sides, into each other's plans.

- Develop integrated B2B sales and marketing campaigns, around an agreed target list, with a co-ordinated programme of activity, specific quarterly objectives and regular reviews of results.

- Set targets, not just for sales, but for all sales and marketing activities, inputs and outputs. In particular, set targets for marketing in respect of lead generation, including the volume of leads and conversion rates from all marketing-related activities (from telemarketing to events). Use your sales database to track performance.

- Adopt more of a project management approach to sales and marketing campaign implementation to ensure high levels of visibility and control.

- Incentivise marketing, just like sales. Bring marketing inside the tent and celebrate its achievements.
- Show leadership from the top, with the CEO getting involved.

See also

Q4   How can we drive our sales and marketing?
Q12   What are the 10 key steps in generating demand?

QUICK WIN MARKETING Q11 What's the difference between sales and marketing?

Q4   How can we drive our sales and marketing?

Here is the result of 20 people brainstorming for 30 minutes on driving sales and marketing – 36 good ideas, grouped under four headings. Why don't you try them with your team?

A. Existing / past customers

- Make contact with past customers.
- Account management – make sure our customers are really satisfied – project reviews with all our clients – re-examine their priorities.
- Up-sell existing customers.
- Get referrals from clients / past clients.

B. How to find potential new customers

- Alliances – co-marketing – potential partners.
- Organise database / buy a database list.
- Memberships, get on the governing board.
- Contact people we have not dealt with.
- Make use of all our contacts (people we know).
- Direct mail / mail-out.
- Networking – going to events.
- More golf (networking).
- Trade missions – overseas markets.
- Telemarketing.
- Check the newspaper, trade press, etc. for announcements.

C. Increase profile and awareness

- Signage at customer sites.
- Newsletter.
- Improve your website – get more web enquiries.
- Blogging.

- Brown-bag sessions on YouTube.
- Get client feedback.
- Advertise.
- Increase the profile of the firm.
- Publicise big / past jobs.
- Get PR – write articles / papers / publish.
- Tell people about your awards.
- Competitions / submissions.
- Talks / presentations.

D. Innovation, new markets, products, etc.

- Look at other markets, or sectors.
- Develop specialised skills in certain areas.
- Develop new areas of business.
- Find new projects earlier (pre-planning).
- Innovate (new products, services, etc.).
- Other services.
- Gather market information.
- Develop new pricing / payment models.

See also

Q3   How can we align sales and marketing?
Q16   How do we prepare for a telemarketing campaign?
Q21   How do I research a potential customer?
Q77   How can we maximise customer referrals?
Q85   What are the key elements of account management?
Q86   What is the difference between account management and account development?
Q89   Why are referrals so important?

Q5   What do we need to know before we launch a new product / service?

You can get insurance for pretty much everything – even very risky activities such as parachute-diving and stock-car racing. But you cannot get insurance for launching a new product or service. Why? Well, because the risks are simply too high.

Here is what you need to know before you decide to launch a new product / service:

- It is going to take a lot longer than you think – and more time and money, too.
- The chances of a set-back, or a false start, are great. There is a risk that your product / service won't get off the ground at all!
- Your plans are how you want it to be and they may be a good guide. But that is not how it will work out.
- If you hire somebody for the job of selling, more than likely they won't work out – success will still depend on you.
- The customers you imagine for your solution are probably not those who need it most.
- People don't know they need your solution; they probably don't even know you exist.
- You need selling more than marketing, because months down the line you will be complaining that you are not getting to see enough potential customers.
- Having the best solution doesn't guarantee success. In fact, nobody cares about your features and technology; what your product does is more important than how it does it.
- People won't believe how good your solution is, unless your customers say so. So don't write brochures, write customer success stories. And that means getting your first satisfied customer as a reference site is key.

- Success is a confluence of factors, many of which are outside your control. Timing is everything.
- Market research may lead you astray, instead of keeping you on track.
- Ironically, the more you think your solution appeals to everybody, the more difficult it will be to market, and the more costly to develop, since you will be tempted to add in more features and more complexity than is necessary.

See also

Q6   How do we start selling in international markets?

We asked managers for their top tips on doing business abroad or entering a new market. Here is the advice they offered:

- Do your homework: What is the opportunity? How big is it? How to exploit it? How long will it take? What will it cost? Overestimating the potential and underestimating the cost / time required is all too common. Relying on market research is just not enough.

- Spend time in the marketplace: There is no substitute for being on the ground and getting to know the people and the market – it is the difference between *knowing* a market and *knowing about* a market.

- Be clear on your proposition / unique advantage in the market: You must understand competitors and how they compare. It is important not to try to be everything, but instead to focus on a few important areas in which you will differentiate yourself. The importance of that first reference customer in the market / segment cannot be underestimated.

- Develop a target list based on a clear customer profile: Don't try to appeal to everyone; instead, target a particular type of customer for whom your solutions have a particular advantage. Search out segments or niches that are most attractive and amenable (for example, least competitive, highest margins, etc.) for your business at this time.

- Test the reaction: It is not *via* research that markets are validated, but by on-the-ground sales activity. Only then will you know, or understand, the requirements of the market and its potential for success. Be prepared to adapt and change your approach based on what the market tells you.

- Localise your approach: What works at home may not work abroad. So:

- Tailor your proposition, adapting your product / service to local needs, tastes and customs.
- Beware of self-reference criteria – people in the local market see things differently to you.
- Do not overlook local differences, as well as customs and traditions.
- Speak the language (even where English is widely used) and have a local telephone number, etc.

- Develop a local partner: Building a base of local contacts is very important, including linkages with complementary service / product providers and, where possible, partnering with a local organisation to overcome the newcomer / outsider objection.

- Adopt a long term view: Make a commitment to the market. Sales cycles are what they are and building relationships is an essential requirement that will take time. Do not let it appear that you have just parachuted in for business today.

- Have a plan: This is essential for setting and managing expectations, clearly focusing energies and resources, assessing progress and generally maximising the potential for success. Planning is not about a document, but about delineating who is doing what and when, as well as the result expected.

- Invest in sales and marketing: 'You get out what you put in' when it comes to time and money spent on sales and marketing – that is, of course, if it is spent well. There is a certain critical mass in terms of the commitment of time and resources to a new market. Delay a decision regarding a new market, or the number of new markets, until management can devote sufficient time and commitment to it.

See also

Q2   Why is it important to take a long-term view in sales?
Q4   How can we drive our sales and marketing?
Q5   What do we need to know before we launch a new product / service?

Q7   Is there a better way to forecast sales than relying on market research?

While listening to the market, and specifically to your customers, is vital, the ability of traditional market research to accurately predict buying intentions is limited. We know this from 10 years of selling market research services to industry and projects involving more than 20,000 interviews with international business buyers and consumers.

It is not about issues of statistical validity, or reliability. But, just because a buyer tells you that he is interested in buying and you tick the appropriate box on the questionnaire does not mean that the buyer actually will buy when your product / service when it is launched. The interviewee is not deliberately deceiving you; it is just that market research questionnaires and real-world buying scenarios are two very different things. We much prefer to base our decisions on sales calls than on questionnaires.

Here are three things you can do to get a more accurate picture:

- The first is get face-to-face with customers – telephone interviews and postal or online questionnaires can only do so much. Make the call more of a sales call, presenting the customer with more information, including prices, visuals, demos, etc. – essential to the customer in making a considered buying decision.

- Even if you are at concept stage, create a visual, or prototype, however simple, that will enable your customer to give a more considered and informed reaction to your product. People have limited time and attention, so make it easy for them to get to the nub of the issue – whether they want your product, what features they really need, etc.

- Ask the right people, at the right time and in the right way – for example, if you want to ask people about domestic appliances, then the best place to do so is in a electrical retail outlet – people there are potential customers and are in the 'buying zone'.

No matter how accurate your picture of the market is, interpretation is everything. Most importantly, scenario-based sales forecasting is key and, in particular, the assumptions you make about the percentages of customers that are actually going to do what they said in the questionnaire and the implications of these figures for your business.

HINT

Base your decisions on sales calls rather than on questionnaires.

See also

Q92   How can we be better at sales forecasting?

SALES
LEADS

Q8   What trends are changing the way sales messages are heard?

Nothing switches a customer off quicker than the traditional sales blurb and marketing speak – promises of superior quality, technical sophistication and service excellence. Courted by an increasing array of suppliers, today's buyer can be hard to reach and difficult to persuade. They are more cynical and sceptical too, capable of quickly consigning your marketing literature to the bin and your sales presentation to history. Increasingly, they are switching off and tuning out.

Fourteen trends are making most sales messages and marketing material less effective and have fundamental implications for the way you sell. Salespeople who adapt will get closer to their customers and farther ahead of their competitors; those who don't, just won't be heard. These trends relate to the audience, the message and the medium.

14 trends that make traditional marketing materials redundant		
	Old Approach	**New Approach**
Audience		
1	Mass market approach	A focus on segments and niches
2	One message for all	A message tailored by segment (CTOs vs CFO)
Message		
3	Features of the product / service	Benefits and results
4	The sales proposition	Reason for the customer to buy
5	Marketing and sales blurb	Useful information, insights, perspectives, etc
6	Long lists of unqualified benefits and product features	Smart lists of quantified benefits, backed up by case studies or customer references
7	How it works	Why it is important (business impact / case)

	14 trends that make traditional marketing materials redundant	
	Old Approach	**New Approach**
8	'Me too' or undifferentiated message	Clear competitive advantage
9	Same old / repetitive message	Messages that are evolving and topical
Medium		
10	Seller talking	Customer talking
11	Supplier says so (partisan information)	Customer or expert says so (third party validation)
12	Old media (print, etc)	New media (PDFs, forums, wikis, etc)
13	Unsolicited message (interruption-based)	Solicited or welcomed (permission-based)
14	What we say	What we do / who we are

See also

Q1 How is B2B selling different?

Q9   Why is strategic focus so important?

Where companies look for growth has a major bearing on the level of success they enjoy – not all markets offer the same potential for growth. Companies that grow fastest do so by choosing carefully where they will compete – they steer themselves strategically into market niches and segments that are attractive and accessible. They may not have the best solution in the marketplace overall, but they do have distinct advantages in meeting the needs of particular groups of customers on whom they focus.

Here are some reasons why you should focus on particular customer groups or segments:

- Your sales and marketing can stretch only so far, so you have to focus your efforts on those customers who can deliver the greatest success. For most companies, 20% of their customers deliver 80% of their profits; this means that too much sales and marketing activity is focused on the wrong customers. One of the greatest opportunities to increase the effectiveness of your sales and marketing is to tailor it to specific segments and niches.

- Some customers are easier to win than others, being more attracted to your solution and more amenable to your sales efforts. Even if everybody needs your product, or solution, there are some that need it more, have specific requirements that only your product satisfies and can pay more for it. So it makes sense to seek them out.

- Every company likes to think that its industry, or segment, is different, so they will ask whether you have done work for others like them. They want to know that your product / solution is suited specifically to their needs. They will listen carefully to hear whether you understand their industry's trends, language and challenges. Being a specialist (or being seen to be a specialist) is important, because customers think the needs of their business and their industries are special.

- A distinctive advantage does not come from being the absolute best, but from being better at meeting the specific needs and buying behaviour of particular customer segments, which vary by sector, location, company size, stage of development, etc. Successful companies have a clear focus on a key market segment(s) where they have a distinctive advantage. Once they choose their ideal customer, they are not afraid to alienate others in tailoring their proposition and message exclusively to their chosen target group(s).

The main reason for getting the strategic focus wrong is an insufficient understanding of potential customers' needs, or of competitors. The next is an impatience to get results, accompanied by a concern that the chosen market may not pay sufficient dividends.

See also

Q2   Why is it important to take a long-term view in sales?
Q10   How do we define the profile of our ideal target customer?
Q20   How do we make sure we only meet people who are prospects?
Q29   How do we position ourselves as experts?
Q46   How do we find out what buyers really want?

Q10   How do we define the profile of our ideal target customer?

Here are some questions to help you decide who you should, and should not, be targeting:

- **WHO?**
  - Who are they?
  - Who (among our customers) are they like?
  - Who are they buying from now?
  - Who can introduce us?
  - Who are they influenced by?
- **WHAT?**
  - What size?
  - What sector, subsector, or niche?
  - What is its ownership, or organisation structure?
  - What do we want to sell?
  - What solutions are they presently using?
  - What solution do they need?
  - What priorities do they have?
  - What success have we had?
  - What references / examples are relevant?
- **WHERE?**
  - Where are they located?
  - Where are they listed, advertising, attending, etc?
- **WHEN?**
  - When is the need at its most (triggers, critical events, etc.)?
  - When is the best time to approach them?
- **WHY?**
  - Why do they need our solutions?
  - What problems, or opportunities do they are have?
- **HOW?**
  - How sophisticated are they?
  - How long are they in business?

- How much can they spend?
- How much competition is there for their business?
- How have we got an edge?

See also

Q10   How do we define the profile of our ideal target customer?
Q21   How do I research a potential customer?

Q11   How do we generate demand?

Your first step in creating demand as a seller is to decide what you want to create demand for. Your second is to decide what fundamental need there is in the target market – business drivers, priorities, strategies, events, and so on – that can be leveraged to generate demand for your solution(s). For example:

- To generate demand for its solutions among companies unaware of the need for such a solution, a supply chain solutions supplier took advantage of a recent food safety scare to highlight the costs associated with meeting food traceability regulations and how its solutions could reduce them.

- An IT supplier surveyed its top customers to predict their IT priorities for the coming year. With security, cost and compliance emerging as key priorities, the company wrote a series of best practice guides in each area and organised seminars to heighten awareness of these challenges and to generate demand for its solutions as a result.

Fundamentally, a basic need must exist – such as the desire to cut costs, save time, ensure compliance, etc. The objective of demand generation is to create awareness of this need and to bring it to the buyer's attention. You must show that the performance of the buyer's business can be improved in a compelling way that the buyer was previously unaware of – and, of course, that your solution provides the best means of achieving that performance improvement.

Last, as in all aspects of sales and marketing, it is important to focus demand generation efforts on the right customer and the most appropriate solution.

See also

Q9   Why is strategic focus so important?
Q10   How do we define the profile of our ideal target customer?
Q12   What are the 10 key steps in generating demand?

Q12   What are the 10 key steps in generating demand?

The 10 key steps in generating demand are:

- Help buyers to evaluate and reassess their priorities by comparing them with their counterparts and peers (for example, 'We asked IT managers about their priorities for next year and here is what they said ...').

- Quantify the problem / opportunity relating to their industry / business, using third party validation to make it credible (for example, 'Industry analysts Gartner put the cost of unlicensed software at up to 30% of software budgets annually ...').

- Show them the results achieved by their peers with your solutions (for example, 'We have helped Company X bring its award-winning new products to market in just 21 weeks using our new system ...').

- Provide useful information not marketing blurb (for example, white papers, blogs, case studies and analysts' reports rather than marketing brochures).

- Talk to those who shape priorities, allocate budgets and make decisions – that means C-level.

- Run educational events, such as talks, seminars and webinars, where customers and experts can talk about industry challenges and how they can be resolved. Key to the success of these events is that they are focused on providing useful information, as opposed to being simply a forum to plug your company and its products / services.

- Position your company as a thought-leader – for example, by writing blogs or articles, sponsoring research, or speaking at events. Seek the limelight by making the topic controversial, using it to provoke and to get people talking about it, thus compelling buyers to sit up and take notice.

- Link your solution with a campaign, or a cause, that already has momentum, ideally something that the customer is passionate about, or something that is topical or 'cool'. It is easier to rally people around a cause than around a product, or a service.
- Enlist the support of others in generating demand – for example, industry associations, experts and so on.
- Sustain your effort over time. Effective demand generation is not just a once-off activity, but an ongoing programme of activity.

See also

Q13 What are the six challenges lead generation must overcome?

The six key challenges lead generation must overcome are:

- Being heard over the noise: Buyers are bombarded with a confusing array of similar-sounding marketing messages from competing vendors. So here is the test – can your sales and marketing message:
  - Grab the attention of marketing-weary buyers?
  - Be heard above the noise of competitors?
  - Enable you to stand out from the crowd?

- Reaching senior buyers: Most purchase decisions rely on the approval of senior managers who are well-buffered from unsolicited marketing outreaches. Most lead generation methods are stopped 'dead in their tracks' by buyers' spam filters, gate-keepers and other barriers erected by buyers. So, can your message:
  - Get through to senior managers?
  - Resonate with senior managers?
  - Get them to engage?

- Providing information that buyers actually need: Most seller messages elicit a 'so what?', or 'what else would you say!' response from buyers, who place little or no value on them. So, here is the test:
  - Are you providing buyers with the type of information they want to receive?
  - Is it is capable of shaping their opinions, or influencing their decisions?

- Shaping requirements and influencing the buying process: Buyers often keep sellers at arm's length until the buying process is well underway. The result is that the seller arrives on the scene only after requirements have been set and a competitive bidding situation has arisen. A key challenge is for the seller to become involved earlier in the buying cycle. So, how successful are your efforts in:

- Shaping the requirements of the buyer and otherwise influencing the buying process?
- Encouraging the buyer to involve you in the early stages of their buying process?

- Creating and sustaining a dialogue: The ultimate test of the effectiveness of any seller marketing is the buyer engagement. However, the response to most marketing is a deafening silence. The challenge is to create a dialogue, to get buyers to opt-in, to participate and to respond, which is how sellers gain the opportunity to really influence buyers and to be top-of-mind when the timing is right. So how effective is your marketing at engaging with the buyer:
  - Is there a reason for buyers to want to opt-in to your marketing?
  - Are you able to sustain an ongoing dialogue?
  - Is your message effective at generating a response?

- Generating demand: It can be a challenge to get the attention of buyers who are searching for a solution. However, those already shopping are greatly outnumbered by those who do not have a budget, or perhaps are not even aware that they have a problem. Reaching this last group presents particular challenges, especially:
  - How to identify those with latent needs?
  - How to generate demand where none already exists?
  - How to spur those who are not yet in shopping mode into action?

See also

Q14   How can we use webinars to advance leads and prospects?

Webinars are a cost-effective means of showcasing your company's expertise and solutions. They can play a role in generating demand for your solutions by educating the marketplace, as well in generating, nurturing and progressing sales leads.

Here is a checklist to help you plan and deliver successful webinars:

A. BEFORE – Planning for the success of your webinar

- What is the objective of the webinar? In addition to showcasing your company's expertise and its solutions, what role will it play in the sales / marketing process for your company? Is it aimed at nudging a select group of sales prospects closer to a decision, building your relationship with existing customers, or generating additional sales leads?

- Who is the desired audience of the webinar? Who do you want to attend? Make a target list from customers, partners and target companies. What companies, sectors and job titles do you want represented?

- How is the webinar to be promoted? Will you email, or write to customers about the event(s)? Will you promote it on your company's web site, in its newsletter, as well as *via* partner, supplier and other industry websites listings and blogs? Can the event be promoted jointly to the membership of various industry and other bodies? What publicity opportunities are available *via* industry magazines and other publications?

- Have a clear structure and topic – a topic of real interest and timely relevance to the target audience.

- Make your webinar interesting and relevant, not just a commercial for your company and its products.

- In preparing your webinar content, ask yourself what three things you want participants to remember when they leave the webinar.

Then structure the material to deliver these key messages with impact.

- Rehearse the webinar with colleagues and get feedback.
- Record the webinar, so that those not able to attend can view it later from a link on your website, or in an email.

B. DURING – Delivering the webinar

- Offer participants the opportunity to interact, ask questions, etc. Let them know if you want questions at the end, or throughout.
- Not too many slides, with not too much text. Ensure a consistent style or layout throughout your presentation (in line with your corporate branding).
- Include a survey at the end of the webinar, this will enable you to measure level of interest, any questions, future topics, etc.

C. AFTER – Post the webinar

- Follow-up after the webinar, so as to get reaction and establish the level of interest, or sales potential. Forward the presentation, or relevant white paper with a thank-you email, or call (whichever is more appropriate).
- Conduct a post-webinar review.
- Have a clear next step in mind for any participants who are sales prospects.

See also

Q11   How do we generate demand?

QUICK WIN DIGITAL MARKETING Q66 How do we run webinars for existing / potential customers?

Q15   How can I make a prospect's PA my sales ally?

Anybody who reaches out to prospects at C-level in large organisations knows that they will talk to many more personal assistants (PAs) and secretaries than to senior executives. However, even very clever sales campaigns can fail to adequately take this into consideration.

Here is the issue: you spend hours training a telemarketing person, or role-playing a telesales script, all the time ensuring that the person making the calls has sufficient product knowledge and understanding to engage the prospect confidently in a conversation. However, your success often depends on your message being communicated third-hand by a PA and in a way that may be completely outside of your control. Your sophisticated message may be reduced to a simple "Gavin called from ACME Ltd. They sell software solutions. If he rings back, will I put him through?".

The PA is the gateway to C-level, the essential conduit for your message. So your message must be distilled to ensure that it can be passed on to the manager easily and still remain intact. By necessity, it has to be a simpler and more pointed message, one that is not aimed at selling your proposition, but on selling the reason why the C-level manager should listen to you.

Here are some tips on how to turn the PA into your sales ally:

- Respect the PA's position: Ask her / him what is the best way of getting information to the boss. Ask when is a good time to call. Ask her if she / he wouldn't mind passing your message on. Ask perhaps if she / he knows whether her / his boss is actually the best person to receive it.

- Don't pressurise and try not to sound like a sales person: Be friendly and polite. Get the person's name, keep it and use it. Make a note of any conversations. When you call back, refer to your previous conversation, so that you don't seem a stranger.

- Remember you are not trying to sell to her, or even to her / his boss: Your objective is simply to exchange some useful information (which, in turn, can lead you closer to selling).

- Provide a reason why she / he should pass on your message or your email: Your objective is to communicate how what you have to say could be of benefit to the manager and to assure the PA that you are not going to be a nuisance (sales) call if you do get put through. So ask yourself how could the manager lose out if he / she does not talk to you or read your information.

- Respect the position of her / his boss too, saying, for example, "I realise that John is probably very busy, but I thought this information might be of value to him because …".

- Gentle persistence: You don't earn the right to get put through on the first call, or maybe even the second. However, keeping in touch with the PA over time means that your name becomes recognisable and your contact will build up a head of steam.

There are many **other techniques**, many of which are more trick than technique. Here is one that is legitimate, however – if you are sending an email, or a letter, then it can be useful to put a note on it saying that you will call. That means you can legitimately say to the PA, "I promised X I would give him / her a call", which distinguishes you from a cold-call.

HINT

The PA is the gateway to C-level, the essential conduit for your message.

See also

Q55   What rules apply to access to decision-makers in the buying process?
Q59   Why is selling to C-level executives different?

Q16   How do we prepare for a telemarketing campaign?

Things only start happening when salespeople pick up the phone and start talking to prospects and customers. It is as simple as that.

However, most organisations do not call enough potential customers, or do it in as systematic manner as is necessary. The lack of prospecting is the number one complaint area for many sales managers. When outside telemarketing agencies are used, the results are often disappointing too. The solution to both these problems is more preparation.

Preparing for a telemarketing campaign involves:

- Deciding who and how many will be called, what the objective of the campaign (metrics, etc.) is and how long it will last, number of days to allocate, setting review dates, etc.
- Building the list.
- Writing out, and re-writing, what you are going to say, until you are happy with it.
- Writing out questions you are likely to be asked and your answers to them.
- Practising what you are going to say and how you are going to say it.
- Deciding what you will say to the PA and what voicemail message if any you will leave (if any).
- Gathering product / industry knowledge.
- Deciding what you will send if somebody wants more information, or what web-page to point them to.
- Preparing the list – agreeing the criteria, finding the names, numbers, ensuring that the company has not subscribed to any 'do not call' list (for example, TPS in the UK), etc.
- Doing your homework on the people and the companies to be called.

- Using a database / spreadsheet to track your calls.
- Allocating time, including uninterrupted slots, in your diary for calling.
- Determining what supporting marketing activity, such as direct mail, will be used.
- Undertaking a pilot (a couple of days of calling in order to test the approach and its effectiveness) before ramping up activity.

Less obvious, but equally important, is the mental preparation required for calling prospects. All too often that gets forgotten about. Yet it is the single most important factor that determines long-term success and failure. In particular, it is key to the ability to sustain sales-prospecting activity, beyond the initial burst of enthusiasm.

See also

Q91   What are the obstacles that prevent individual salespeople selling more?

Q17 How can we use LinkedIn for business development?

You may have heard it said that what matters 'is not what you know, but who you know'. Yet, few people consider themselves to be good at networking. But, social networking, once the reserve of teenagers, has reached the business world and provides business networking with a real shot-in-the-arm.

Everybody has heard of the 'six degrees of separation' – the notion that there are only six people between you and anybody that you could want to contact. Now LinkedIn, the professional equivalent of Facebook and Bebo, shows businesspeople that they are better connected than they think.

LinkedIn is essential for every professional – whether they want to find new customers, to build their professional profile, to find out about a company, to recruit staff, or to look for a new job. It enables most people to effortlessly double, triple and quadruple the number of contacts to which they have access. In fact, it will quickly provide access to thousands of new trusted contacts. The word 'trusted' is important because, unlike cold-calling, these people are linked to you by somebody they have worked with, studied with, or done business with in the past.

Here is how it works:

- Sign-up for free and enter your career and educational history – it is a little like preparing your CV, only that you are guided step-by-step online.

- As you build your profile, you will be presented with other members who have worked in the same companies and studied in the same institutions (in the same time-period as you). You can choose to link yourself to them. When you do, they will receive an email asking them to accept a link from their profile to yours.

- You can import your contact list from Outlook (or another source) to LinkedIn, which will result in an even longer list of people to whom you also might be linked. Again, you can select any of the automatically-generated contacts and they then receive an email requesting a link to you.

Two things determine the strength of your profile on LinkedIn: how many connections (or links) you have to others and how many recommendations you have received. The latter is a direct result of how many others you give recommendations to, and is well-controlled: before a recommendation from another person appears on your profile, you get to view and approve it.

If you want to sell to a new company, for example Company XYZ, you can search for the company and see whether there is somebody in that company who either you know directly, or you know through somebody else. You can view their profile and contact them by email. You can also contact a certain number of people directly even if you don't have any links (part of the paid service).

You also can join groups on topics that are of interest (for example, ERP software), where you can share thoughts and opinions with other members. You may be interested in joining groups that your potential customers might be interested in.

What are you waiting for?

See also

Q21   How do I research a potential customer?

QUICK WIN DIGITAL MARKETING Q16 What is LinkedIn?
QUICK WIN DIGITAL MARKETING Q48 How do we make connections on LinkedIn with people we don't know?

Q18   How can we generate more enquiries from our website?

How well your website performs in terms of generating leads and enquiries for your business is largely in your own hands:

- Restructure your site and rewrite your website text to reflect the key words you have chosen. That means renaming pages to correspond with the keywords, changing headings in the body and writing copy itself that includes them.

- Add links to your site from sites of similar content and request back links to your site from others. To do this, you could add your name to various internet directories or join a links exchange. However, it is the popularity or quality of links to your site that matters, not the quantity.

- Add content that is interesting, relevant and fresh. Transform your site from an online ad, or brochure, to a source of valuable information for potential visitors. Use this content to contribute to blogs and other sites. Put articles, opinion pieces and white papers on to various portals and sites.

- Register your site with Google and other search engines and keep registering it on a regular basis. Submit a site map.

- Add a blog or forum, again packed with the right keywords and back-links and actively submit to third-party forums, adding back-links to your own pages.

- Add more stuff. Use a newsletter with links to your site. Add a You Tube video by taking your company's sales presentation and adding a voice-over. Add your company to Wikipedia, LinkedIn and so on. Also adding FAQs to your site can be effective.

- Experiment with buying a certain number of clicks, or visitors, to your site. When you buy from Google Adwords and others, you need only pay for visitors to your site, as opposed to for the showing of your ad, so it can be well worth doing.

See also

Q17   How can we use LinkedIn for business development?

QUICK WIN DIGITAL MARKETING Q90 How many visitors to our website do
we need to make one sale?

Q19 How should we nurture contacts?

The new approach to pre-qualification requires adopting a longer-term perspective on the potential of any target customer. Although a prospect may not contribute to this quarter's target, they might do so one or two quarters out. But how will you nudge these could-be customers along effectively and efficiently, while you are chasing those already in your pipeline and in shopping mode?

The answer is a programme of nurturing that involves one-to-one contact through your marketing, for example:

- Week 1: Send a white paper (not a brochure)
- Week 6: Call to invite to an event, or webinar.
- Week 12: Send a clipping from a magazine, or press release.
- Week 16: Ask whether they would like an executive briefing on a relevant topic.
- Week 24: Ask whether they would like to talk to one of your gurus or experts about a new area.
- Week 25: Send a customer success story in the post.
- And so on.

Then your marketing does your pre-qualification for you. You will determine who is genuinely interested, while educating your prospects along the way and nurturing them to sales readiness. All the while you have built the relationship, demonstrated your commitment and hopefully, based on the quality of the engagement, shown your company to be an expert in its industry.

See also

Q2   Why is it important to take a long-term view in sales?
Q29   How do we position ourselves as experts?
Q36   How can we get the prospect to do our pre-qualification for us?

SALES MEETINGS

Q20   How do we make sure we only meet people who are prospects?

'I don't want to meet tyre-kickers' is something we often hear from salespeople. The next sentence always is 'I want to meet with people who have got a problem and are looking for a solution'. All that makes sense.

However, when it comes to ensuring that you only meet with people who are real prospects, you need to:

- Have a clear definition of your target market / customer and a list that carefully matches it: If a company is not the type of company that you should be meeting, they should not be on your target list at all.

- Put in place a process for nurturing leads to the point where they are ready to meet a salesperson: Too many salespeople rely on the sales meeting as their first – and their last – point of contact with a potential customer. However, rather than meeting with every company that is a lead, or a prospect, you need a Plan B. You need to have something to send, a reason to call back to the person in a number of months, perhaps some event that the person can be invited to, etc. – all alternatives to the face-to-face meeting and all designed to nudge the company along to the point where meeting a salesperson makes sense.

- 'Kiss some frogs ...': Increasingly, we find that buyers are slow to divulge their needs and wants, especially to a cold-calling salesperson. If you really want to understand the potential of a target customer, a face-to-face meeting is essential. Here is the important point, however: even if the company does not have the potential to buy today, they may well have the potential to buy in the future. That means keeping in touch with people you have met is vitally important.

- Do more preparation in advance of sales meeting: For example, researching both the company and the people to be met. This will inform your judgment as to the potential application of your solution to the company, as well as ensuring that you are meeting the right people (that is those at a sufficiently senior level).

- Sell to those without budgets: If you are in a sales cycle and the potential customer does not have a budget for the purchase, then you have a real problem. However, you cannot only meet those who have a budget and are shopping for a solution. You must be open to exploratory conversations and must adopt a longer term view, meeting with the right companies and working to shape their future priorities and budgets. In this way, you generate demand for your solutions – albeit long-term. This also means that it is important for you to meet with the senior managers who have the power to allocate resources.

See also

Q10 How do we define the profile of our ideal target customer?
Q19 How should we nurture contacts?
Q21 How do I research a potential customer?
Q22 What preparation do we need to do before a sales meeting?
Q35 How do I know whether a prospect represents a genuine sales opportunity?
Q55 What rules apply to access to decision-makers in the buying process?
Q59 Why is selling to C-level executives different?

Q21   How do I research a potential customer?

Your effectiveness in matching your company's solution to the prospect's needs, demonstrating your professionalism and generally making an impression on the prospect, can be increased greatly by researching the company in advance of your visit. That means getting information on the company, its products and its industry, from the following sources:

- The company's own website.
- A Google search for other online references to the company (it may be useful to set up a Google alert on the company name).
- Your company's own sales database.
- Colleagues, friends and contacts.
- The prospect's annual report and company accounts, if relevant.
- Trade and professional associations.

What information will be useful to you in preparing for, as well as during, your sales call? Here is a checklist:

- What size are they? How long are they in business?
- What products / services do they offer? What is their core technology?
- What are their markets and who are their customers?
- Do they compete on price? Quality? Service? Delivery?
- What are the key opportunities and challenges facing the company and its industry?
- How are they performing at the moment? What is their financial situation?
- What is their organisational structure and who are the key people in the company?
- Who is likely to be involved in the purchase decision and what are they like?
- What recent events (product launches, recent appointments, etc.) have taken place in the company?

- Who do they presently buy from? What are their procedures with respect to suppliers? What are they like to deal with? Do they pay on time?
- What past work has your company done that is specifically relevant to this company?

You need ALL this information before you meet your prospect face-to-face, so you don't waste valuable meeting time in information-gathering.

See also

Q10   How do we define the profile of our ideal target customer?

QUICK WIN MARKETING Q34 What are Google Alerts?

Q22   What preparation do we need to do before a sales meeting?

To be prepared and maximise the chances of success, follow these straightforward steps:

- Confirm the meeting, including who is to attend.
- Clarify expectations for the meeting (for example, format and agenda).
- Do your homework on the company and its industry.
- Research the person(s) you are meeting (for example, role and background).
- Prepare relevant customer stories and insights.
- Prepare a list of questions to ask.
- Prepare answers to questions and objections you will be asked.
- Pack sales aids (for example, reference letters or financial statements).
- Decide what you want the buyer to think, say and do after meeting.
- Consider the next step for both parties.

See also

Q23   What are the top 15 customer questions and how should I handle them?

Q28   What can I do to make sales meetings more effective?

QUICK WIN MARKETING Q16 How do we prepare for client meetings?

Q23 What are the top 15 customer questions and how should I handle them?

You have delivered an excellent sales presentation. The prospect is impressed and has lots of questions to ask. But are you ready? Give the wrong answer and the sales opportunity may evaporate.

Here is a list of the top 15 questions that buyers ask in relation to high-value B2B solutions. Rehearsing the answers, adapted to your context, will help you to impress the customer by increasing your level of comfort, credibility and effectiveness during the sales process.

When the customer is exploring alternatives:

- Why should we choose your company?
- What are the advantages of your solution over other methods / approaches / products / services?
- Why is it better than your competitors'?
- Why should we do it now, as opposed to next year? Why shouldn't we do it in-house?

When the customer is looking for confidence:

- Has the product / service been bought by others in our industry?
- Do you have an office in our market / territory / region?
- How strong is / what financial backing has your company?
- Has the product / service been tested, verified or certified by any independent organisation?
- Can this solution be tested / piloted? Is there the possibility of a pilot / proof of concept?

When the customer is looking for a cost-benefit equation:

- Our business is different ... how can this solution work in our business?
- I question your figures ... can they really be achieved?

- Can the benefits be substantiated?
- What is the return on investment?
- What is the cost?
- Why is it so expensive? What is the total cost of ownership (including installation, maintenance, training, etc.)? What is the payback on the investment?

Of course, then there is likely to be a range of questions relating to details of your proposition, such as: How does it work?, Is it compatible with?, How long does it take?, What skills are required?, What about ongoing maintenance?, Upgrades?, Support?, etc.

The more questions a potential customer has for you, the better – it shows he / she is interested. However, in a sales presentation, even an expert can stumble if presented with a complex, or difficult, question. Relying on *ad lib* answers to questions is not enough. The true sales professional creates a list of all the questions, or objections, likely to be received and carefully prepares their responses.

So start with the list above. Add any other objections or questions that you, or your colleagues, have been asked and keep adding to the list over time. Then write out your response, rehearse them and put them in a folder that can be used by any new salesperson joining your team.

> **HINT**
>
> You should make a list of all the questions, or objections, you are likely to receive and carefully prepare your responses.

See also

Q28 What can I do to make sales meetings more effective?
Q32 What should we do to make sure of a great sales presentation?
Q57 How do we differentiate ourselves from other suppliers?

Q24   Should we be honest with the customer – always?

Salespeople are often caught in a difficult position when it comes to being completely honest with the customer. For example, the buyer asks about certain product functionality that is not yet available. The functionality is under development, or it will be developed if the customer signs the order. However, the buyer has asked a straight-forward question, "Does the product do A?". How should you answer?

You could tell the truth and potentially sabotage the sale, or you could lie and answer, "Yes, it does". Nine out of 10 salespeople do the latter – and then get found out!

Stop taking chances on being found out. Stick to the truth, regardless of the consequences. Surprise the buyer with refreshing honesty – which the buyer is likely to repay with trust and respect.

We saw just how powerful this can be in a presentation by one of our clients recently. The prospect had set out a list of requirements and asked competing vendors to present their responses. Our client's sales director listed not just the requirements that could be met immediately (some 60% of the total), the requirements that would require minor customisation (a further 25%) and the requirements that would require software code development (the remaining 15%). He also listed the dependencies, addressing upfront the key project risks (such as integration with third-party systems), the steps to mediate risk, examples of how this had been achieved in previous projects, and so on. What a breath of fresh air! It immediately indicated trustworthiness and credibility.

Try it for yourself, the next time you're tempted to say "Yes, it does".

See also

Q27   What is it buyers want to hear?

Q25   What's the difference between 'leads' and 'contacts'?

The term 'leads' – sometimes called 'prospects' or 'suspects' – means different things to different people. For some, leads are simply raw names on a target list; for others, they are people who have engaged with the business (for example, by registering on a website, or demonstrating interest on a cold-call). It's confusing.

But, more importantly, the term 'leads' and all that is associated with it is outdated; it's no longer sufficient to ensure a sustainable sales pipeline. Quite simply, yesterday's lead generation methods do not generate enough sales opportunities, particularly high quality opportunities. They are not enough to lure increasingly sophisticated buyers. However, not only are they inadequate of themselves, but they are overused and abused. Typical of this is the growth in the volume of generally unwelcome cold-calling and email marketing, which is short-term in focus – 'we need leads this quarter to fill our pipeline' – rather than working towards building a relationship and creating a dialogue.

While both leads and contacts are aimed at generating sales meetings with potential customers, the latter is the more contemporary and sophisticated method. Some of the differences are outlined below:

Leads ...	Contacts ...
Generated and prequalified.	Nurtured.
Require a campaign.	Require a conversation.
Are fed a sales pitch, or elevator scripts.	Are provided with useful information and insights.
Typically, start-stop, *ad hoc* and re-actionary.	Developed and nurtured on an ongoing basis.
Short-term focus – get the meeting / sale.	Long-term view – relationship / dialogue.
Go stale.	Last forever.

Leads ...	Contacts ...
Small number of sources.	Multiplicity of sources.
Typically, poorly organised.	Live in a database / CRM system.
Traditional marketing focus.	Underpinned by a relationship marketing approach.
A cost.	An investment.
Often, interruption-based.	Permission-based.
Based on sources that generate lower conversion rates and less predictable results – advertising, cold-calling, etc.	Emphasis on sources that deliver greater returns and higher conversion rates – introductions, networking and referrals.

See also

Q11   How do we generate demand?
Q12   What are the 10 key steps in generating demand?
Q13   What are the six challenges lead generation must overcome?
Q19   How should we nurture contacts?

Q26   Why should we 'stop selling'?

'Stop selling!' may sound like strange advice, especially to salespeople. However, the reality is that most salespeople perform at their best when they stop selling. When the pressure to sell is removed, salespeople begin to listen more closely to their customer's need and prospects start to open up about what they want. As a result, the chances of sales success are increased.

So, if you find yourself selling, here are some guidelines to follow:

- Stop being a salesperson: Be an expert and trusted advisor instead.

- Stop talking about your company and its products: Focus instead on the challenges and opportunities facing your customers. Stop listing features and benefits, talk about business impact instead.

- Stop pitching, and start listening: Stop doing all the talking, get your customer / prospect to engage.

- Stop trying to control meetings: Get an interesting dialogue going and let the customer take you where he / she wants to go.

- Stop assuming the customer needs your solution, or saying your solution does everything. Explore instead the opportunities, challenges and strategies of his / her business.

- Stop looking only for people who are ready to buy: Start creating the need for your solutions and helping prospects to become aware of previously hidden needs or solutions.

- Stop closing: Instead, help the customer to create a compelling reason to buy.

- Stop taking a short-term view: Look ahead to the next quarter and afterwards to develop a keep-in-touch, or relationship, mindset with prospects who are not ready to buy today.

- Stop writing and emailing proposals: Start writing your proposals alongside the customer and arrange a time to discuss them once delivered.

- Stop sending brochures: Send an interesting white paper, or article with more interesting and useful information.

Although this advice may appear radical and new, it is not. It appears in the first chapter of the highly influential 1989 book, *New Strategic Selling*, by Miller Heiman – and it's as valid today as it was then.

See also

Q2 Why is it important to take a long-term view in sales?
Q13 What are the six challenges lead generation must overcome?
Q19 How should we nurture contacts?
Q29 How do we position ourselves as experts?

Q27   What is it buyers want to hear?

Most salespeople think that buyers want to hear about their company, its products and services. They assume that buyers are interested in their features and benefits lists, as well as their competitive advantages over competitors. These faulty assumptions result in a lot of sales pitches, presentations and proposals that miss the mark. The reality is that buyers are not really interested in these things at all.

Buyers have heard it all before – the promises, the product claims, the glowing self-praise – and, as a result, are slow to accept it. They want to hear not your sales speak, but rather the words of your customers and the results they have achieved with your products or services.

It is time to tell buyers what they want to hear and spare them from all the rest. That means it is time to tell buyers how you can help them. More specifically, how your products and services will help them to solve a particular problem, or exploit an opportunity, they are facing.

Buyers want to talk results and little else. This is the reason they sit up and pay attention to sellers who quantify results and back them up with third-party validation.

If results are the answer, then 'Why should I buy?' is the question. But before you get to that point, there are lots of other questions:

- Why should I click (on your web link)?
- Why should I listen (if you call)?
- Why should I enquire (if I read your ad)?
- Why should I meet with you?
- Why should we meet again?
- Etc.

See also

Q24   Should we be honest with the customer – always?

Q28   What can I do to make sales meetings more effective?

Here is what sales people are doing to make their sales meetings more effective:

- Present later in the sales cycle and only when you have a full understanding of the customer's requirements: Of the many types of sales meetings, the least effective (particularly at the early stages) are sales presentations, where the sales person is expected to present details of his / her company and product, often using a slide-show.

- Demo later and do it better: Doing a demo too early generally means you are less in control of the outcome, including managing customer expectations. Presenting a demo before the customer's business drivers, product requirements, background, etc. are established makes it difficult to ensure that your demo hits the mark. It often results in demos that focus on features, as opposed to benefits.

- Talk less and listen more: If you talk more than 50% of the time in any sales meetings (25% in initial meetings), you have a problem. You should spend most of the meeting time listening, since that is the only way you can establish needs, build rapport, etc.

- Ask more questions and better questions: Questions that illuminate the customer's wants and needs, criteria, decision making process, etc. Questions that invite direct answers, even if they are negative, 'Is this a good time for you to consider this solution?', 'Is this price range within your budget?', or 'Have you ever done business with a company of our size before?'. Questions that prequalify the customer in terms of budget, authority, timing and need.

- Do a more structured needs analysis: Take the customer systematically through a process of clarifying business needs and priorities to identify unanticipated needs, to build understanding, consensus and dynamics for change, and to uncover hidden motivations, understand personal and political motivations and develop a quantifiable business case.

- Tell more stories of how other customer have benefited from your solutions: Focus on the impact on the performance of their business. Customer success stories, when validated, have a greater impact than almost any other marketing material.

- Set expectations and agree realistic objectives: What do you want to get out of the next sales meeting? What is the customer expecting? Too often, salespeople go to a sales meeting expecting to sell, while buyers arrive expecting (and not wanting) to be sold to. Managing expectations is key – for example, you might say 'I'd like to listen to understand your requirements and then I will go away and formulate some ideas that we could discuss at a future meeting, and then prepare a proposal if that makes sense ...'. Having a clear next step in mind (another meeting, documentation, etc.) is important.

- Prepare, plan and pre-qualify: A meeting that lasts for an hour, if it is to be effective requires two or more hours for preparation, follow-up and follow-through.

- Take better notes in meetings and more systematically follow up the people you have met. Adopt a keep-in-touch, or relationship, mindset.

- Work better as a team: Too many cooks spoil the broth; the same is true of selling. When working with another salesperson, make sure you both work well together, that you both are clear on roles (who leads the meeting) and on what areas / questions you each will address, that you agree how you will communicate with each other during the meeting (a signal to suggest moving on, etc).

- Stop selling and start acting like an expert: That means adopting a consultative approach, helping the customer to uncover problems and explore solutions. Demonstrate your expertise and knowledge of not just your products, but also the customer's industry / business / challenges and how they are being addressed by others.

HINT

Customer success stories, when validated, have a greater impact than almost any other marketing material.

See also

Q29   How do we position ourselves as experts?

Consider:

- Experts outsell salespeople every time: The level of expert knowledge is the key factor differentiating high-performance sales people from the rest.

- The demise of the salesperson: Buyers increasingly are sceptical of salespeople. Experience has taught them not to believe everything (anything?) they are told, nor to rely on a salesperson for insight, information, or expertise.

- The rise of the expert: Nobody wants to be sold to. Yes, people need to buy things and making the right choice is more and more difficult. But, for most buyers, the fewer salespeople they have to meet, the better. That's because most salespeople make the buyer's decision more, rather than less, difficult. Experts, on the other hand, are always welcome.

- New job titles don't make experts: Where salespeople were re-packaged as 'consultants', 'advisors', or 'specialists', little else changed and buyers were not fooled. Titles alone don't change the salesperson's level of product and industry knowledge, credibility in the eyes of the buyer, or ability to 'get down and dirty' in solving customer's problems.

Making the transition

From 'salesperson' to 'expert advisor' is a small change in words, but a major change in attitude, skills levels and sales approach. Salespeople begin to walk taller when they see themselves as an expert. They also begin to act a little differently. Buyers begin to act differently too, engaging more, listening more and trusting more.

The expert must be able to:

- Identify customer needs, some hidden, by asking good questions.

- Consult and engage with the customer being sufficiently confident and knowledgeable to advise, educate, persuade and inform.

- Demonstrate knowledge, without appearing as a show-off, or 'know-it-all'.

Product knowledge is not enough

The number one complaint of buyers used to be lack of product knowledge. But product knowledge is only part of the expertise equation. Knowing the product and in particular how it works, is not today's buyers' primary interest. Instead, they want to know how your solution will help their business to meet its specific needs and challenges.

The first step is to become an expert in your own solutions and how customers use and benefit from them. From there, the next step is to become an expert in your industry and your marketplace.

Are you an expert? Take the test:

- Does the customer see you as qualified to help and advise them, or simply as somebody trying to sell something?
- Do you know the customers' industry, its opportunities and challenges? Have you taken the time to understand their business and its strategies?
- Can you tell the customer how others have benefited from your solutions and in detail how they are using them?
- Do you have some insights, or information that is not available otherwise to the buyer?
- Have you had enough product training? Are you certified?
- Have you read leading research papers on the industry and the technology in question?
- How visible is your profile as an expert? Have you written something, joined a professional body, or given a talk?

See also

Q24   Should we be honest with the customer – always?
Q27   What is it buyers want to hear?
Q30   What questions can we ask to help identify buyers' needs?

Q30　What questions can we ask to help identify buyers' needs?

The following questions will help you to identify and address a buyer's needs:

- What does the buyer want to achieve?
- What does the buyer's company want to achieve?
- What are the key business drivers in this area?
- What is the underlying opportunity, or challenge facing the business? How big is it? How urgent is it?
- What is the context in terms of the organisation's history, culture, politics, etc?
- What is the gap between desired and actual performance in the area in question? How does this compare with internal and external expectations?
- What are the relevant industry drivers, or trends?
- Are there any critical events, or dates, to be taken into account?
- Who does the opportunity / challenge impact on most? How? Who else is affected? In what ways? What are the consequences? What is the cost?
- Has the impact of the opportunity / challenge on the business been quantified? In a credible manner? What are the relevant metrics? How will success be measured?
- Is this area a priority? If it is, why has it not been addressed to date (constraints)? If the issue has been addressed / discussed in the past, what happened?
- What are the competing priorities and projects?
- How does this opportunity / challenge fit with existing people and processes?
- What are the barriers – internal / external – to addressing the challenge / exploiting the opportunity?

- What could prevent this moving forward?

See also

Q29 How do we position ourselves as experts?
Q31 What questions should we ask in an early-stage meeting with a buyer?
Q46 How do we find out what buyers really want?

Q31   What questions should we ask in an early-stage meeting with a buyer?

Remember the buyer owes you nothing, and that includes answers to your questions. As a salesperson, you have to earn the right to ask questions and so you must build the trust that will encourage buyers to answer freely and in detail.

Focus more in early meetings on how you can help and, in particular, on the information you can share, rather than the information that you want. A salesperson who shows up at a meeting with a standard product-led sales pitch and a list of questions to determine needs and facilitate his / her sales process pre-qualification will be seen by buyers as self-serving and worthy of being left waiting in the hall. The objective of a first meeting should be to share some useful information with the buyer – for example, an insight into what his / her counterparts or competitors are doing, the challenges they are facing and the results they are achieving. After all, that is the most powerful way of communicating the benefits of your solution. Here is an example:

We have worked with A, B and C to achieve X, Y and Z and, based on these projects, we have ... noticed an important trend ... identified a range of key success factors ... identified a number of factors that are often overlooked ... employed a new way of ... achieved some surprising results ... etc.

So, the questions you ask in the meeting logically relate to that insight shared, to those challenges, benefits and trends discussed. For example:

- Do you think this (insight) is relevant? Have you seen this trend yourself?
- Who does it affect in your business? How does it affect them?
- Is this something that you would be interested in exploring a little more? What aspects of it in particular?
- How important do you think this could be? Do you think it could be a priority? For when?

- Other companies have faced challenges in implementing (budget, time, other priorities, etc.). Do you think these would apply here?

- Has this issue been examined before? If 'Yes', what was the outcome? If 'No', is there a reason why this issue has not been addressed before?

- What would you like to do next? Is there anybody else in your organisation that would be interested?

See also

Q29 How do we position ourselves as experts?
Q30 What questions can we ask to help identify buyers' needs?

Q32   What should we do to make sure of a great sales presentation?

When it comes to delivering a presentation, preparation is everything – even for the most polished of presenters.

Here is a checklist to help you to ensure a great sales presentation:

- What is your objective for the presentation?
- Who is in the audience? How many people will be present?
- What are they expecting?
- How much do they know about the topic already?
- How cynical, or sceptical, will the audience be to your message? What opinions do they have?
- What is the message you want to communicate?
- How are you going to make it accessible and interesting?
- What stories, anecdotes, or case studies are you going to use?
- How much time have you got?
- How do you want to be introduced?
- What three key ideas do you want the audience to talk about afterwards?
- What, if any, formalities need to be adhered to?
- What size is the venue? What is the seating layout?
- What equipment will you have (audio / visual)?
- How much interaction will there be?
- How much preparation and practice will you need to undertake?
- Will slides be used? How many?
- What set-up time will be required on the day?

See also

Q28   What can I do to make sales meetings more effective?

Q33 What follow-up should we do after a sales meeting?

Sales champions adopt a keep-in-touch mindset for all their valued leads and contacts, nurturing them to sales readiness and increasing their own chances of success where a future sales opportunity does arise.

Most sales meetings do not present immediate sales opportunities. At best, they offer the vague promise of a future distant need, or perhaps no promise at all. Perhaps there is a competitor already entrenched, or no available budget; even more frustrating, maybe you know they need your solution, but they just can't yet see it. Bottom line, you leave the meeting knowing that the prospect is not ready, willing, or able to buy.

Most sales people, although disappointed, pick themselves up and move on enthusiastically to the next sales meeting. Maybe *that* will be the one that uncovers a real sales opportunity. If not, then perhaps it will be the one after that. As salespeople, we turn for comfort to the law of averages, which tells us that if you meet enough prospects, you will stumble eventually upon the one who is ready and in the buying zone. It keeps us going and it also keeps us busy, but it often results in the neglect of relationships as salespeople fail to keep in touch with the scores of prospects once met and quickly forgotten about.

High-performing salespeople keep in touch with the entirety of their contact base, with the level and frequency of contact determined by a rating scale reflecting the potential associated with each company and contact in their sales system or database. For example:

- They send an occasional email newsletter, article, or information piece to those that represent 'long shots'.
- They diary a periodic telephone call, be that every six weeks or three months, as appropriate.

Good intentions are not enough. A CRM system is required to schedule the periodic ongoing contact, to make it easy to administer and to ensure that it does not rely on the vagaries of memory.

To avoid follow-on contact falling into the nuisance category, ensure that the communication has a real value. For example, send:

- An article or whitepaper that might be of interest.
- A note regarding a move by one of their competitors.
- A link to a website containing useful information, etc.

Nurturing companies and relationships over time to sales readiness is essential to long-term sales effectiveness. It recognises that, in most situations, needs are latent and await discovery, which may take weeks, months or even years.

Sales meetings and sales leads are simply too expensive to be discarded because they don't produce an immediate opportunity. If the company in question qualifies for your target list, then you should want to keep in touch, helping to generate awareness of the need over time and being there when the need is recognised. Even if the result of all the nurturing is not a sales opportunity, it can still be worthwhile, as a source of useful information, referral or introduction to others, etc.

The reality for most salespeople is that a keep-in-touch mindset, or approach, has the potential to double, if not triple, sales success in the long-term. A first pass of a target list in terms of leads generated and meetings held will result in a certain number of sales opportunities and, ultimately, sales wins. However, a programme of progressive contact with the same target list over time will deliver twice or three time the results of a once-off campaign. That is why business development requires a strategic approach.

See also

Q2   Why is it important to take a long-term view in sales?
Q19   How should we nurture contacts?
Q28   What can I do to make sales meetings more effective?
Q84   How do we become more pro-active in managing customer relationships?
Q93   Why do we need a sales system?

SALES CYCLES

Q34   What is the sales cycle?

The sales cycle includes everything from the initial sales meeting to the point of writing a proposal and closing the sale. Most importantly, the sales cycle is where the seller helps the buyer to buy.

One of the key lessons for all of us in sales is that you cannot miss a step. When it comes to a complex sale, you cannot go straight from an enquiry, or an initial sales meeting, to writing a proposal.

The sales cycle is the essential meat in the sandwich of the sale. It is the most important aspect of the sale and an area that, for most sales teams, presents the greatest potential to boost sales success.

When buyers rush to write a proposal, to close the sale and to negotiate a deal, their chances of success are drastically reduced. They do not have enough information, or influence in order to win the sale. They are likely to be oblivious to:

- How the decision is going to be made (the buying process).
- Why the decision is going to be made (the business logic, or business case).
- Who is going to make the decision (the buying team).

During the sales cycle, the buyer goes a full 360 degrees from little, or no, understanding of these items, to a full understanding of and engagement in respect of all three. The sales cycle is the process of matching needs to solutions and building relationships and trust in the process.

Only when this is complete is the salesperson primed to write a winning proposal and close the sale.

See also

Q38   What questions should we be asking buyers at different stages in the sales cycle?
Q44   How can we shorten the sales cycle and accelerate the sale?

Q35 How do I know whether a prospect represents a genuine sales opportunity?

No salesperson wants to waste time with tyre-kickers who cannot buy. However, prequalification can present many challenges.

Traditional prequalification follows the BANT acronym:

- Is there a Budget?
- Does the manager have the Authority to make the purchase?
- Is there a clear and compelling Need?
- Is the Timing right?

However, there are now two important additional dimensions to pre-qualification:

- You must sell to those who don't have a budget: In a difficult marketplace, salespeople cannot sell only to those who have a budget allocated to the purchase. They generate demand for their solutions among those who have not yet allocated a budget to the purchase, or perhaps may not even be aware of the solution. Getting involved earlier in the sale, before the budget is allocated, greatly increases your chances of success. If you wait until buyers are ready to buy, then you risk being called into a competitive bidding situation, which will be much more difficult to win. This means you must adopt a longer term view, being prepared to meet with and nurture a relationship with prospects who cannot buy this quarter, or perhaps even the next.
- You need to fully understand the buying decision: What is required in order for the potential customer to be able to buy. Specifically, you must understand:
  - The buying process: All the steps, information and analysis required for a decision to be made.
  - The business case: The business logic for the purchase, centred on the 'benefits – costs x risk' equation.

- The buying team: Everyone who will be involved in shaping and making the buying decision (from the user, to the senior manager who will sign it off, and everyone in between).

Evaluating the prospect of a sale using these criteria elevates pipeline and opportunity reviews to the level of a science. The key issue becomes not 'Can we make the sale?', but 'Can the buyer make the purchase?'.

See also

Q20   How do we make sure we only meet people who are prospects?
Q41   How can we help the buyer to buy?
Q43   How does a seller's views of a solution differ from the buyer's view?
Q46   How do we find out what buyers really want?
Q52   Does one-to-one selling work?

Q36   How can we get the prospect to do our pre-qualification for us?

How you allocate your time as a salesperson is key. In particular, maintaining a healthy pipeline requires that you balance your efforts between:

- Focusing on closing the most likely deals for this quarter.
- Nurturing those prospects with potential for next quarter.
- Generating fresh leads to go in at the top of the sales funnel.

To get the balance right can be a challenge. Key to the efficient use of your time is a system for pre-qualifying prospects and opportunities on which you are going to focus. But, too often, pre-qualification is applied in a blunt manner. Applying the popular BANT (budget, authority, timing and need) criteria too rigorously to an inbound enquiry or cold-call could exclude the bulk of the marketplace, including many companies that do not have a budget for your solution now, but still represent potential customers.

As well as selling to those who are already actively searching for a solution in the marketplace, every sales organisation must generate, and foster and nurture, demand for its solutions. That means sales and marketing must work together, with marketing substituting for pre-qualification at the lead generation stage. While some leads are classified as sales, or sales meeting-ready, others not ready for the next step are not left to waste but are nurtured. Later in the sales cycle, pre-qualification becomes more important, as the time and resources you must commit to an opportunity increases. Progressive pre-qualification – that is, asking the right questions – ensures that you can adapt your sales approach continually (if you are talking to the wrong people, or addressing the wrong requirements) to ensure you have the maximum chances of success.

Pre-qualification, like all aspects of selling, is not something that is done *to*, but rather is done *with*, a prospect. It must be a two-way process – that means asking the customer what stage he / she is at and what they want to do next, if anything. It is important to remember that you have to earn the right to ask progressively more direct and searching questions.

Your approach should reflect the stage of the buying cycle (if, indeed, there is one) that you are both at, as shown in the table below, ideally incorporating as many buyer-focused questions as possible.

Stage	Pre-qualifying questions	Seller-focused questions	Buyer-focused questions
Sales LEAD	Should we be talking?	Do you fit the profile to be on our target list? Have I got something that is interesting for you?	I am not sure if this is of interest to you ...
Sales MEETING	Should we meet?	Is it mutually beneficial to meet at this time? What useful information or insights do I have to share?	Is this something that is important to your business? Is it an area for which you are responsible?
Sales CYCLE	Should we explore problems / solutions together? How should we engage?	Are you at the exploration of, needs, solutions, or suppliers stage? What is the need? What is the ideal solution? What is the buying process? Am I talking to the right people? Am I getting the right reaction? Do I have a sponsor? How am I positioned? Where am I strong? Where am I weak? What is the next step?	Is now a good time to look at this? What are the implications of the problem? Is there a reason why this problem has not been addressed to date? How does it fit with your organisational priorities and strategies? Who else needs to be involved? What would the ideal solution look like? What are the alternatives? What are the constraints? What are the characteristics of the ideal supplier?

Stage	Pre-qualifying questions	Seller-focused questions	Buyer-focused questions
Sales ORDER	Can / should you buy / buy from us?	What is the business case? What are the selection criteria? Are there any orange or red lights?	
REPEAT Sale	How strong is our relationship? Can, or should we deepen it?	How are we performing? How well are we working together? How can we help more? What is the sales / profit potential?	

See also

Q11 How do we generate demand?
Q12 What are the 10 key steps in generating demand?
Q28 What can I do to make sales meetings more effective?
Q34 What is the sales cycle?
Q35 How do I know whether a prospect represents a genuine sales opportunity?
Q47 How do we establish the customer's buying criteria?
Q49 How do we get a good understanding of what motivates the buying organisation and its key people?
Q56 What should the business case look like?
Q76 Why are customers lost?

Q37   What are the implications of the client's cost of the buying process to me as a seller?

The cost of selling to an organisation is only a fraction of the cost of that organisation's buying decision. For example, where a major buying decision involves three competing suppliers, the time that the seller spends with the buyer has to be multiplied by 3 if the buyer allocates one-on-one time to each of the suppliers involved.

For example, suppose the buying process takes six months to complete, involving five managers for one hour per week over that period. Based on an annual salary cost (including some overhead allocation) of €100,000 per manager, the buying process could cost the buyer as much as €45,000. Add more managers, or more time per week, and the cost spirals.

This has a number of implications for sellers, including:

- The decision to engage in the buying process, in itself, is a significant commitment of resources by the buyer. For this reason, it is generally made in stages, with the sponsor in the buying organisation first being required to present a justification for a buying decision and a business case being prepared.

- Only a limited number of projects can be evaluated at any one time. This means that, although a project is of interest, the timing may not be right. As a vendor, you must show buyers how your project can impact on their immediate business priorities.

- Given the cost and time required, organisations will want to 'kill off' poor projects as early as possible. You may have to do most (or all) of the initial running for a project to gain traction.

- Organisations are standardising their approach to buying decisions, including steps to be followed, templates for documents, etc. This makes the process more repeatable and consistent, thereby saving time for them. You need to know – and follow – the approach required.

- Involving another supplier in the process costs time and money, so don't expect to be able to squeeze in late when you hear that a project is under consideration, even if your solution is ideal.

- Buyers want to limit the time / cost of the buying process, which means being judicious about time spent with sellers. When you want access to all the stakeholders, you need to be conscious of the fact that this represents an additional draw on their time and adds to the cost of the decision.

- Buyers want to get something back for the time spent with vendors. They may need to meet with three vendors because their internal process requires three vendor quotes but, if each vendor requires 20 to 40 hours of time (including briefings, presentations, proposals, ongoing communication, etc.), it's understandable that the buyer wants some immediate payback.

- Once a vendor has been selected, it makes sense for the buyer to want to develop and deepen that relationship, as opposed to going through the entire process again. When customers defect to another supplier, they face real switching costs related to the process of evaluating, educating and learning to trust another vendor.

See also

Q35   How do I know whether a prospect represents a genuine sales opportunity?

Q40   What must we do to win the sale?

Q38   What questions should we be asking buyers at different stages in the sales cycle?

The questions depend on the stage you are at. Asking the wrong questions at the wrong time can present problems for both buyer and seller. With this in mind, here is a summary of some of the questions that are relevant at the different stages of the buying cycle (note the use of the term 'buying cycle' as opposed to 'sales cycle').

Stage	Objective	Questions
Contact	Nurture	Should we be in contact? Do they fit the profile? What needs might they have? What information do they find useful? Should we meet?
Meeting	Explore	Should we be talking? Is this of interest? What else might be of interest?
Cycle	Engage	Should we engage (can we help)? How to engage (help)? Who else should we engage with? What is the need? What is the ideal solution? Who is the ideal supplier? How and when will the decision be made? Is there a budget allocated, etc?
Orders	Business Case	What is the business case? Is it compelling? What are the costs, benefits, risks and constraints?
Repeat	Client Success	How are we impacting on your business? What are the metrics? Will you recommend us to others? Can we help you tell the story of your success? How can we help you further?

A word of caution: don't spend precious time with the prospect gathering information (for example, number of employees, product range, etc.)

that can be gathered in other more efficient ways (such as from the company's website).

Similarly, limit the time spent on form-filling type questions, as opposed to questions aimed at building and demonstrating understanding, interest or empathy.

See also

Q19   How should we nurture contacts?
Q21   How do I research a potential customer?
Q31   What questions should we ask in an early-stage meeting with a buyer?
Q34   What is the sales cycle?
Q47   How do we establish the customer's buying criteria?
Q56   What should the business case look like?
Q79   What are the main barriers to repeat sales?

Q39   'To speed up the sale, you must slow down'. What does this mean?

Uncertainty in the marketplace has brought longer sales cycles, which have implications for meeting sales targets and sales costs, as well as for the overall level of visibility, predictability and control in respect of sales.

To improve win rates in a tough market, sellers have to revisit the timing on their sales pipeline and adjust the timing of their 'conveyor-like' sales processes. Specifically, you should slow down in the following 10 ways:

- Before you diagnose the solution: You have seen the situation hundreds of times before and can see the problem clearly, but slow down so to ensure that you understand all the nuances, as well as the political and organisational context.

- Before pre-qualifying: In a market of buoyant demand, salespeople were eager to pre-qualify early so that they could spend their limited time with those who represented the greatest prospect of a sale. Market conditions now mean that, for every customer who is ready to buy, there are eight or nine who have the potential to buy but are not ready to do so yet – they may not even be aware that they have a problem. So replacing pre-qualification that identifies those ready to buy with marketing that nurtures those who can and perhaps should buy, but are not ready, is key.

- In your first meeting: Too many salespeople still aim for the one-meeting pre-qualification and even one-meeting close. However, increasingly, they are being boycotted by buyers who want to go at their own pace because, for buyers, it feels too much like they are being 'sold to'. Realise that you cannot understand a buyer, his / her needs, or his / her business in one meeting, just as you cannot build a relationship, or establish trust in that 45-minute time-frame.

- Before proposing a solution: Take time to understand the buyer's full needs, to explore solutions jointly, to build rapport, etc.

- Before asking too many questions: You have to earn the right to ask questions, especially sensitive ones. You have to be willing to share information with the buyer, before he / she will return the favour.

- Before delivering a presentation: Take time to understand your audience's needs and interests. Put your laptop and presentation slides aside and have a conversation – see where it takes you.

- Before writing a proposal: The earlier you write a proposal, the more assumptions you must make regarding the customer's needs and wants. Getting the customer involved in writing the proposal with you may mean that you have to move the opportunity out by a quarter, but it dramatically increases the likelihood of success.

- Before starting to negotiate: Good negotiating cannot compensate for bad selling. Negotiating on price, for example, before the needs have been fully understood, the solution defined, or the business case demonstrated is meaningless and inadequate.

- Before moving on to your next customer: Buyers complain that the attention – sometimes, excessive attention – they receive during the sales process quickly diminishes once the order is won.

- When you see an orange or red flag: If you are too focused on getting the deal across the line, you may be blind to warning signs, such as not being able to get access to the decision-maker(s), not having all the information needed, the issue of price arising too early, etc. However, orange and red flags are to be welcomed, particularly when identified early in the sales cycle – in time for the underlying issues to be addressed, or for you to walk away.

See also

Q40   What must we do to win the sale?

A professional salesperson is a student of buying. They know that the success of a deal depends on understanding not only how the buying decision will be made, but also the business decision that underlies it.

Here are 10 of the most important questions that salespeople need to answer in respect of each opportunity in their pipeline to increase their chances of success:

Questions	Implications to be considered
1. Who are all the stakeholders?	Do we understand the requirements of all stakeholders, not just technical, for example? How can we ensure access, without by-passing agreed channels?
2. Who are all the decision-makers and influencers?	Have we had contact with all the decision-makers? Do we understand their personal, as well as business, drivers? How are we positioned with each?
3. Is there a clear definition of requirements?	Is the requirements definition clear? How has it been gathered? Is it complete – are there needs that we can additionally address? Has it been validated? Have requirements been prioritised, with any contradictions and trade-offs addressed? Does the weighting of requirements reflect our strengths and minimise our weaknesses, or can we influence it to do so?
4. What is the buying process? What are the key steps? How long will it take?	How sophisticated is the buying process? What stage is the prospect at now: > Recognition of need? > Search for a solution? > Selection of supplier?
5. What about competing projects (that includes 'do it in-house')?	Are there competing projects for the same budget? Could the project be delivered in-house? Could the project be delayed till next quarter, or next year? What factors will determine the selection of these options?

Questions	Implications to be considered
6. Is a business case required? What format will it take? Who will write it?	Can we provide information that will help build the business case, in terms of costs, benefits and risk (including implementation)? Can we include a model to quantify benefits and total cost of ownership?
7. What is the role of procurement?	Have we had contact with procurement? Do we understand their requirements?
8. Is there a shortlist of vendors? How many? What are the criteria?	How do we rate on the shortlist criteria? Can we help shape the criteria?
9. At what level is final sign-off required?	If this project requires board level sign-off, for example, how will this impact on selection? How does our proposal connect with strategy? Has our proposition been CEO-proofed? Can we have access to / inform board members in advance of the decision?
10. Who is in the role of business analyst (the bridge between technical and business, whose role it is to create the business case)?	Who has this responsibility? If there is no separate person (for example, the Operations director is creating the business case), then this raises issues regarding how the proposal will be reviewed at board level, for example.

So, for each opportunity in your pipeline, ask each of the questions outlined above, considering the implications of your answers for your next steps in managing that opportunity to the point of closing.

See also

Q41   How can we help the buyer to buy?
Q56   What should the business case look like?
Q65   How can we boost win rates?

Q41   How can we help the buyer to buy?

You can help the buyer to buy (from you) in the following ways:

- Start learning about the customer's business and industry.
- Start listening, instead of talking.
- Start collaborating with your customers in exploring solutions for their business.
- Start sharing insights and telling stories of how your other customers are tackling challenges and exploiting opportunities.
- Start asking better questions, not just to gather information about the customer's business (particularly if that information can be got from other sources) but to understand the opportunities and challenges facing his / her business.
- Start inputting to the business case. Since the buying decision is first and foremost a business decision, you should be talking more about the business logic and underlying numbers for the purchase, as opposed to your company's unique selling points.
- Start building a relationship, even if the prospect does not represent a potential sale for this quarter.

See also

Q42   What mistakes will buyers not forgive?

Professional buyers have heard it all before, which makes them less forgiving when salespeople make any of the following mistakes:

- Not knowing enough about your own products, or the customer's industry: This is buyers' number one complaint about salespeople.

- Suggesting we need your solution without taking time to research our needs, or requirements: It is risky to assume the customer has a problem and needs your solution, so don't forget to ask first.

- Claiming that your solution meets every company's needs and failing to appreciate that my business / challenge(s) is different.

- Talking as if yours is the only option, making us suspect that you want to sell to us regardless of suitability.

- Hinting that the customer does not know what they are doing, or that what he / she is doing is wrong. Surprisingly, this is quite common, with many sales pitches beginning with a statement such as '80% of software projects are over budget', 'most IT inventories are out by as much as 20%', etc., which can be seen as thinly-veiled insults to the customer.

- Oversimplifying the customer requirements: For example, suggesting easy integration with third-party systems, when buyers know that integration is never easy.

- Making exaggerated claims that detract from the credibility of their message: For example, 'reduces time to market from months to just hours', 'cuts integration costs by up to 90%', or 'can be implemented for just 10% of the cost of traditional solutions'. Your claims must be believable and backed up by customer references.

- Getting defensive if the customer questions your solution, or not attaching enough importance to objections and questions raised.

See also

Q41   How can we help the buyer to buy?

Q43   How does a seller's view of a solution differ from the buyer's view?

Not surprisingly, sellers are very good at talking about their solutions; after all, they know (or should know) the features and benefits of their products and services off by heart. However, the seller's view of the solution and that of the buyer differ in five key ways:

- Can't see the alternatives: The buyer has a range of alternative solutions beyond that of the seller, including doing nothing, doing it in-house, adopting another technology, supporting a competing project, etc. As a salesperson, you must consider the full solutions set available to the buyer and place your solution in that context. Increasingly, the real competition you face is not another vendor, but another project, technology, or strategy.

- Confusion about the source of value: The buyer and seller can have a different view of the features and benefits of the solution that are most important. For example, a market research company may promote the scientific nature of its research techniques as a key selling point; however, for the buyer, the ability to make decisions based on the information gathered is key and so the buyer is likely to want to talk to business analysts and consultants ahead of statisticians. When you list features and benefits, stop to ask the buyer how important these are and why. This will enable you to provide the buyer with more of what he / she is prepared to pay for and less of the rest.

- Key success factors are not clear: In meeting his / her business needs, the buyer knows that the seller's product or service is only one element of success; there are also people and process dimensions to the overall solution. For example, a financial services company that purchases the latest back-office solution, complete with new features and technologies, knows that the impact of this technology is likely to depend less on how good it is and more on how well it is implemented. Managing a programme of change around the adoption of your solution will have a major bearing on your success as a seller.

- The total project view: Your solution is only one element of an overall programme or investment by the buyer. For example, a client was negotiating the sale of its financial services solution, valued at almost €8 million, as part of a larger €120 million project into the buying financial institution. Knowing where its solution fitted in a complex project resulted in:
  - The seller being able to offer lessons from projects of similar scale.
  - The potential to run certain phases of the project concurrently, thus eliminating areas of overlap and creating the potential to share resources (in respect of testing, for example) across a number of phases of the project.
  - A full appreciation of business drivers, constraints and the dependencies for the project overall.
  - An understanding of how other aspects of the project could impact on the success of the seller's implementation.
  - The identification of a number of project partners with whom relationships should be developed.
- Confusion about scope: We advise clients to include a 'Scope' section in their proposal documents, to spell out clearly how both parties will know when the project is complete. Agreeing what is inside – and outside of – the scope is critical in managing scope creep as the project progresses.

However, the most common mistake in matching the buyer with a solution is to fail to understand fully the buyer's needs. Buyers only want solutions because those solutions fix a problem, or meet a need. It is not how a solution works, which is where sellers focus, but the benefits that matter most to buyers. Unless you focus on benefits that clearly address the buyer's needs, you run the risk of getting the solution wrong, in any one (or more) of the five ways listed above.

See also

Q23 What are the top 15 customer questions and how should I handle them?

Q42 What mistakes will buyers not forgive?

Q44 How can we shorten the sales cycle and accelerate the sale?

Sales managers dream of shorter sales cycles, but the reality is that, to speed up the sale, they may need to slow down their selling.

Trying to accelerate the sale, without accelerating the underlying buying decision is futile. The buyer will not be rushed into making a decision and any pressure to make this happen is likely to reflect very poorly on the seller. So it is vital to have realistic assumptions regarding the length of the sale.

Until the steps and requirements of the buying process have been followed, a compelling logic for the purchase (typically, in the form of a business case) has been established and all those who must be engaged and consulted have been involved, the sale cannot be accelerated.

Your ability to accelerate the sale is directly related to your ability to help the buyer to buy and, in particular, to build a compelling business case to buy now, as opposed to buying later.

A sales cycle that is progressing slowly needs more interaction, not less; requires more time, not less; and may require retracing some of the earlier steps. And, if a buying decision is stalled, there is no option but to go back to basics: understanding the buying decision, reappraising needs and exploring solution alternatives.

See also

Q2 Why is it important to take a long-term view in sales?
Q34 What is the sales cycle?
Q41 How can we help the buyer to buy?

Q45   How can we use problem identification to sell?

The savvy salesperson knows that he / she must identify problems, while at the same time protecting people. For example, he / she must get to the heart of problems in the warehouse without directly criticising the warehouse manager. This is at the core of influencing people.

Here are some techniques that will help you to sell your solution, while at the same time avoiding resistance on the part of the prospect:

- Tell stories to help customers understand their own situation. This enables you to couch comments and observations that may be relevant to the prospect's business in a neutral third party way.

- Have a good sense of politics and timing. Know the right time to speak out about problems and how loudly to do so. Earn the right to speak, by your demonstrated level of expertise, credibility and trust. Don't speak until invited (even tacitly) to do so.

- Ask questions, rather than making statements. Use them to steer the customer along the path of greater awareness and to help them arrive at their own definition of the problem. Focus your questions not just on the problems, but on the implications and possible solutions. Probe behind the facts to understand how people feel about the situation.

- Listen and empathise as a means of demonstrating commitment and building rapport. Encouraging the customer or prospect to open up about his / her problems and challenges is the supreme test of a salesperson's skill. The prospect has to feel that, by opening up, he / she is not simply providing you with ammunition to be used in a subsequent sales pitch.

- Focus on the positive, as opposed to the negative, and on opportunities, as opposed to challenges.

- Compliment your customer: It is important to find out about the company's successes, strengths, achievements, etc. and highlight these in your conversations and your proposals.

- Choose your language carefully: What one person sees as 'benchmarking', another may consider 'fingerpointing'. When you use words such as 'review', 'assessment', 'audit', clients and prospects may translate these terms crudely into 'you think you know it all', or 'you think you are better than us'.

- Be careful when you are using analysts' reports and statistics: They can be a blunt instrument, being used in most cases to infer a problem in the prospect's company, or industry and to deliver a negative message. Statistics are no substitute for a full understanding of the customer's business.

- Put yourself in your customer's shoes: There is a wise Spanish proverb that says 'It is much easier to talk about bulls, than it is to step into the ring'. Don't judge a person, or a situation, until and unless you are in that situation yourself. For those directly confronted with a problem, there is a level and complexity that the outsider cannot immediately appreciate.

See also

Q46   How do we find out what buyers really want?

Q46 How do we find out what buyers really want?

Buyers don't buy products or services; they buy solutions to problems, or the ability to exploit opportunities. Whichever they do, they do so to meet a need. So why do sellers spend nine times more time on average talking about their solutions than the needs of the buyer?

Here is how you identify – and then meet – the needs of the buyer:

- Avoid premature diagnosis of the solution. Allow the buyer to define the problem before you prescribe a solution. Don't make assumptions regarding the customer's needs, or even that he / she needs what you are offering.

- As an expert, you may know the problem and even may be able to identify the solution immediately. However, take care to involve the customer in this discovery, building trust on the way. This requires a consultative approach, with the salesperson adopting the role of an expert, or trusted, advisor.

- Understand what stage the buyer is at:
  - The need is hidden (blissful ignorance).
  - The need is recognised.
  - They are actively looking to resolve a recognised need.

- Understand the company and its industry, as well as its goals and strategy. Without this, you will struggle to understand the buyer's motivations, the trade-offs, constraints and complicating factors that bear on their needs and the needs of the other stakeholders involved in the buying decision.

- Don't take the buyer's needs on face value. Dig beneath the surface. Look to the implications of the needs. Help the buyer to develop a clearer picture of his / her needs and the advantages of solving them (using your solution).

- More questions are not the answer. Ask better questions – questions that relate to needs and their implications. Don't ask situational questions – for example, about the size of the company, how long it was established; that information is 'nice to know' as opposed to 'need to know', and can be found easily from other sources (such as the company's website).

- Buyers can be slow to open up. When they hear questions, they fear closing. As a seller, you must earn the right to ask questions. You do this by showing tact, a willingness and ability to help.

- It is not enough just to listen and to understand needs; you must provoke, inspire, enthuse and engage with the buyer around the opportunities and challenges facing their business.

- You must help the buyer envision life after the problem has been solved. 'No pain, no sale' was the old sales philosophy, with the salesperson's job being to find and accentuate points of pain. However, the sales professonal moves beyond the pain and the problem to focus on the benefits, the vision, the business impact and the likely risks that will need to be overcome.

- Sell to those with latent needs. The role of the salesperson now includes demand generation, which means that traditional pre-qualification criteria no longer apply.

- Sell higher in the organisation – where priorities are set and new budgets can be created in response to needs identified. This will require a new vocabulary and a new message, as well as confidence and skill.

HINT	Buyers don't buy products and services; they buy solutions to problems or the ability to exploit opportunities.

See also

Q45   How can we use problem identification to sell?
Q47   How do we establish the customer's buying criteria?
Q49   How do we get a good understanding of what motivates the buying organisation and its key people?

Q47   How do we establish the customer's buying criteria?

It sounds simple, but the best way to find out the buyer's buying criteria is to ask. Having said that, however, there are some complicating factors:

- An understanding of all aspects of how the buying decision will be made is required to make sense of the buying criteria. Specifically, you need to understand:
  - The buying process: All the steps, information and analysis required for a decision to be made.
  - The business case: The business logic for the purchase, centred on the 'benefits – costs x risk' equation.
  - The buying team: Everyone who will be involved in shaping and making the buying decision (from the user, to the senior manager who will sign it off, and everyone in between).

- The buying criteria depend on the stage of the buying process – the criteria for short-listing will be different from the criteria for final selection.

- Buyers increasingly are keeping their cards close, so it can be a real challenge to get the buyer to open up and reveal the true nature of the decision they are going to make. To really understand how the decision will be made, including what can be complicating and conflicting factors, often unspoken, depends on the salesperson earning the trust of the buyer.

- Buying criteria are only part of the story: Selecting a supplier is not the greatest challenge facing buyers. Buying decisions don't stall because buyers cannot choose a supplier; they stall because the buyer has failed to establish a compelling rationale, or business case, for the purchase. Important buying decisions are first and foremost business decisions, so you must be as concerned about the criteria for the business decision supporting the purchase as about the competitive advantages of your solution.

- You must seek to influence the buying criteria: Perhaps there are needs that the buyer has overlooked or there are extras that can be provided, etc.

See also

Q46   How do we find out what buyers really want?
Q48   What if the buying criteria set are not favourable to our company?
Q52   Does one-to-one selling work?
Q56   What should the business case look like?

Q48 What if the buying criteria set are not favourable to our company?

If the buying criteria are not favourable, then you have three choices:

- Seek to change the criteria in your favour.
- Carry on regardless and hope for the best.
- Decide that you should walk away.

Obviously, the first is the most desirable option – that is to influence the buying criteria. So ask yourself:

- Can new criteria be added to reflect areas of strength for your company and its proposition?
- Can criteria weightings be changed, so that areas where your company is at a disadvantage are relatively less important in the overall decision?

In considering these questions, it is useful to look at influencing buying criteria on four levels:

- Needs: The definition of the business need, or criteria for business success in respect of the purchase. For example, the business need may be to reduce administrative costs by 10% over 16 months. It is in addressing this fundamental business need / driver that you have greatest leverage in respect of shaping buying criteria.

- Solutions: The definition of the optimal solution and the criteria used to narrow the range of alternative solutions being considered. For example, the buyer may have defined a solution to its software needs in terms of buying an off-the-shelf solution, or custom coding, and set the requirements accordingly. However, perhaps the buyer has overlooked other options and prematurely arrived at a solution definition. This may present opportunities for you to introduce software as a service, or a managed service, as options in an attempt to change the buying criteria.

- Supplier: The criteria for selection of the supplier(s) to provide the solution. This is where you spend most of your time as a seller, yet it is the area where it can be most difficult to make ground. For buyers, the competitive advantages of one supplier over another is subsidiary to the definition of the need and the solution.

- Success: The criteria for the ultimate success of the purchase, including delivery or implementation and everything that has to happen post-purchase to ensure that the results anticipated are achieved. Increasingly, this has an important role in shaping buying criteria and is an important area where sellers can shape requirements.

Shaping the buying criteria is the supreme art of the salesperson, although it is a skill that appears to be in decline because salespeople increasingly are called upon later in the buying cycle, when the requirements have been set. So, it is important for you to become involved in the buying process earlier, often before a buying process has even begun.

See also

Q41   How can we help the buyer to buy?
Q47   How do we establish the customer's buying criteria?

Q49   How do we get a good understanding of what motivates the buying organisation and its key people?

What do you need to really understand what is driving the buyer? Well, here is a step-by-step formula:

- Go beyond features to benefits and then keep on going, because buyers are not as impressed by benefits lists as sellers like to think they are. Benefits are a hypothesis about what is important to the buyer, a catch-all list of possible reasons to buy – but that's all they are. Most benefits and features lists are too long, laden with adjectives and are vague, unquantified and subjective. Often confused with features, benefits tend to be written with the technical, as opposed to the business, buyer in mind and generally do not reflect the issues of concern to senior management.

- Go beyond selling solutions and then keep going. Too often, salespeople start selling a solution before they understand the problem, or need, that it is meant to solve for the customer. Here is the problem – buyers don't really want what you are selling! Instead, they want the results that it can help them to achieve. The challenge of moving beyond the solution can be made more difficult by some customers, when they send out an RFP, or request a proposal, without giving the salesperson an opportunity to really understand their needs (often, the buyer has a less than complete understanding of his / her needs).

- Go beyond the pain and the problem to the results. It is fashionable to talk about point of pain for the buyer as the fundamental motivation to buy and, in particular, as providing the impetus to buy now. This is one step up, in terms of intensity, from the focus on the problem as a means of selling your solution. However, while both of these elements are important, an even more compelling approach is to focus on what your customer is trying to achieve. That is the hope, as opposed to the pain; the opportunity, as opposed to the problem. So, what is the business impact of your solution? Specifically, how will it impact on the productivity, performance, revenue and profit of your prospect? How will it impact on other key business metrics?

- Go beyond results and keep going until you get to the strategy. With buying decisions being made higher and wider in most organisations, there is still one common denominator for senior buyers – business strategy. Sales people must connect with managers, not through the focus on solutions, problems and pain, but instead on their strategy for their business. That is what they want to achieve and perhaps your solution can make it a reality. Selling at a strategy level can present a challenge for many salespeople, because it requires a new level of insight, as well as a new language – one that is more akin to businesspeople than traditional salespeople. It marks the transition from salesperson to trusted advisor and requires deeper relationships, as well as high levels of credibility and trust.

See also

Q50 How can we change our language / approach to meet buyers' needs better?

You know the song, 'You say "tomato", I say "tomatoe" – let's call the whole thing off!'. Buyers sometimes feel that way when dealing with salespeople. For example, when it comes to looking at orders and how they are won, vendors are concerned with proposals, negotiation and closing, while buyers are concerned with costs, benefits and risks / constraints. As a result, sellers write proposals that don't reflect the information that buyers must present in order to get the purchase approved.

Take, for example, the structure of the typical vendor proposal, compared to the structure of the buyer's business case, or purchase approvals document:

Vendor Proposal	Buyer's Business Case
Introduction	Introduction
Problem	Strategic rationale
Solution	Alternatives:
Benefits & Features	Costs
Cost	Benefits
Team, Company &	Risks & Constraints
Credentials	Recommendation
	Implementation

Take this further and look at some of the headings and terms buyers are likely to use in writing a business case – take the guidelines for seeking central government funding for UK road projects:

- Current situation
- Problems
- Exclusions
- Assumptions
- Future situation
- Objectives
- Risks
- Actors / stakeholders
- Scope
- Targets
- Tolerances
- Assessment of alternatives

- Sensitivity analyses
- Benefit Cost Ratio (BCR)
- Project Plan

- Consultation & participation
- Non-monetised impacts
- Constraints

- Option testing
- Cost estimate robustness
- Deliverables

How widely used are these terms in sales proposals? Not often enough. Which leads to the question: How valuable is the content of your sales proposal in helping the buyer in getting his / her project approved and in building the business case?

See also

Q46   How do we find out what buyers really want?
Q49   How do we get a good understanding of what motivates the buying organisation and its key people?

Q51   How can we win over buyers in a downturn?

The economic downturn has resulted in budgets being slashed and many key projects being delayed, postponed, or even scrapped. As a consequence, how organisations are buying and implementing solutions has changed, with important implications for the way organisations are selling.

To win over buyers, your sales message must show clearly:

- An immediate payback: Most customers are delaying making decisions on any project that cannot demonstrate an immediate pay-back. They want to see results fast, and they won't just take your word for it. They need evidence or, more to the point, justification that is both quantified and verified.

- Reduced cost: There is widespread re-negotiation of contracts, with customers seeking to cut back on rates, project days, etc. With fewer new projects starting and increased vendor competition, you have little choice but to agree to customer requests for cost reductions.

- Sharing the risk: You must consider risk / reward-based pricing in order to revive stalled projects. But how do you reduce uncertainty about the level of risk, or the likelihood of reward – you need ask yourself this question.

- Zero tolerance for project over-runs, or delays: Tighter control of spending, and more disciplined project management of initiatives, has given renewed emphasis to agile methodologies of project delivery, including regular iterations, or releases.

- Phased implementations: Increasingly, cash-strapped and risk-averse customers are looking to break down major initiatives into bite-size chunks that are both easier to manage and easier to fund.

- New licensing models: In this era of IT cost-cutting, anything goes. Vendors are 'going back to the drawing board' with software / hardware investment, service rates and the timing / staging of licensing renewals all under review.

- Point solutions: In this present climate, few managers and directors are out to change the world, or even their major systems. The focus has turned to point solutions that will solve an immediate pain. Of course, these solutions must easily integrate with existing and future technologies.

- An end to the 'big vendor' bias? 'We only buy HP or IBM' is something that vendors hear less of these days. The trend towards consolidating all technologies with a single vendor is dead, as budgets are not there for it at present.

Q52   Does one-to-one selling work?

One-to-one selling is a thing of the past. Now, if you are selling to an organisation, most purchase decisions involve between four and six people. In a time of greater risk and uncertainty, the numbers involved grows, with some research suggesting a 16 percent increase in the last year alone.

The bad news, of course, is that more people involved means longer sales cycles and more complex buying processes. Bottom line, it means more uncertainty for the salesperson, as well as lots more work. At its simplest, more people involved in buying decisions requires more meetings and presentations. So, if you still selling one-to-one, then you are neglecting the other people who may determine whether you get the order.

Here are some questions to establish whether your sales approach covers the full buying unit:

- Has the buying group been identified? Has it been covered? Just as there is a team involved on the buying side, sales people need to adopt a team-based approach to selling. In particular, you should be selling executive-to-executive, matching the different members of your team to the relevant person in the buying organisation – for example, your CTO talking to their CTO, etc.

- Are you selling high enough in the target organisation? Does their contracts manager know you? Has there been contact at CEO, CTO, COO, etc. level? Are your contacts sufficiently senior? Take care that your sales proposition resonates with senior management, for whom feature-led messages are not of interest. Generally, selling higher requires a change of language and emphasis to focus on business impact and the business case for your solution.

- Are you selling wide enough? Have you a clear picture of who will make and influence the purchase decision, as well as all those who will be affected by it? Have you had sufficient contact with these various individuals – the economic buyer, the technical buyer, the business driver, the end user, etc? It is important to tailor your approach to each level and each function – for example, the CTO requires a different type of information and approach from the CFO.

- Do you have an internal 'advocate' or champion? Have you identified the internal champion for this project in the customer's company? Does this person regularly contact you for information and advice? Have you built a strong relationship of trust with him / her? Conversely, who has the potential to sabotage your sales effort (perhaps because they feel threatened)? How can this threat be managed?

It is dangerous to assume that you know who is going to make the final purchase decision. It can mean that you focus your sales efforts on the wrong people, or overlook some of those who are important.

See also

Q59   Why is selling to C-level executives different?

Q53 What is relationship selling?

Most complex sales are predicated on relationships – that is, your ability to build rapport, credibility and trust with the buyer. Yes, buyers want the best solution, but that solution is not always the most feature-rich or functionally-sophisticated product.

For what use is a great product, if you don't know and trust the people who are going to help you to implement it? Time and again, companies buy on the basis of people and company, ahead of product or solution.

When we talk about the relationship between buyers and sellers, we talk about three dimensions; height, width and depth. If you are planning to close a deal any time soon, then you need to be sure that you rate highly on each:

- Height: Are you talking to people at the right level – that is, C-level (CTO, COO, CEO, etc.) and have you got their attention and respect? Have you 'CEO-proofed' your message, tailoring it to address the key business drivers of concern to senior managers (costs, sales, etc).

- Width: Are you talking to all the right people – that is, covering the buying group, including the decision-maker(s), economic buyer, technical buyer, user, etc. Do you really know and understand the requirements and concerns of each? Have these been adequately addressed?

- Depth: How deep is the respect, trust, credibility and rapport you have earned? Are you seen as a salesperson, or as an expert? Are you seen as a trusted advisor? How open is the buyer with you, and *vice versa*? How much time and genuine interaction has there been? Has there been any contact outside of formal meetings, or interactions? Have you demonstrated a genuine commitment to helping the customer?

Sales people and their managers find it very useful to analyse both existing accounts and sales opportunities along this revealing three-dimensional relationship scale.

Although the focus has changed from transactions to relationships, the way we sell has been slower to change. Relationships cannot be fast-tracked – an investment in building relationships requires a long-term view (well beyond the next sales meeting, or this quarter's sales target). The era of the one-meeting sale is long over.

> **HINT**
>
> Work on building the relationship needs to happen long before a request for a proposal is received.

See also

Q2   Why is it important to take a long-term view in sales?
Q19 How should we nurture contacts?
Q29 How do we position ourselves as experts?
Q54 How can we fast-track our company's credibility for sales purposes?
Q59 Why is selling to C-level executives different?

Q54 How can we fast-track our company's credibility for sales purposes?

Credibility is an essential ingredient of getting the sale. It is the stuff that buyer confidence is made of. Credibility isn't a problem if you can point to 70 reference sites, a global brand and a million-dollar balance sheet. However, for younger companies, it can present challenges.

Here are some ways you can fast-track your credibility and increase your sales ability as a result:

- Become an expert and specialist: It is hard to be credible and the best at everything, so specialise when building your expertise.
- Ask for, and use, customer recommendations. Put them on the first page of your website.
- Join an association or, even better, get on its governing council.
- Start a blog, or join a blog – to build your credentials online.
- Talk at an event, or seminar – and tell people you have done it.
- Create partnerships: Link to others to build your own credibility.
- Add a heavy-weight to your board: Having a statesperson figure as chairman can add serious credibility.
- Write a book, paper or article: It is easier than it sounds.
- Create an advisory panel: If you sell banking software, form a banking advisory panel with luminaries from industry.
- Get an award or accreditation for yourself, or your business.

See also

Q29   How do we position ourselves as experts?
Q53   What is relationship selling?
Q77   How can we maximise customer referrals?
Q89   Why are referrals so important?

QUICK WIN MARKETING Q37 How do we win awards?

Q55 What rules apply to access to decision-makers in the buying process?

Access to stakeholders in the buying-decision process is a privilege, not a right. If you are fortunate enough to get access, here are the rules you must follow:

- Always obey the rules regarding access; don't go over or around others to get to who you want.
- In order to ensure you access the right people, map the buying process to the organisational chart to identify who you need to meet. Then pair it with your team as appropriate (for example, their CFO to your CFO).
- Tell them why you want to meet, ask them what they want to get from the meeting and set a clear agenda in advance.
- Take advantage of other forums for interacting with managers of interest – for example, industry association events, conferences, etc.
- Use access sparingly and plan to get the most from any time you have with stakeholders. That includes meeting at the right time and when the value of doing so is at its highest. Make sure you have your initial briefing, or scoping, completed first.
- Do your homework in advance. Make sure you are fully prepared (don't waste time gathering information in the meeting that you could have found from the company's website or annual report).
- Research the person(s) you are going to meet, to understand their role, their previous positions, their qualifications, any contacts that you have in common, etc.
- Consider the use of workshops that have a value to the buyer as a means of making access efficient – for example, a workshop on defining requirements, completing the business case, etc.
- Make sure meetings and presentations don't go on for any longer than they need to.

- Provide the buyer with useful insights or information to aid the decision-making process.
- Provide tools and templates to support eliciting requirements, defining the specification, building the business case and making the business decision.
- Be judicious and tactful regarding the questions you ask of the buyer. Remember that you have to earn the right to ask questions that may be seen as invasive, or sensitive.
- Always get permission to include the company in your marketing in the future.
- Always make a point of expressing your gratitude for the time you have been granted by the buyer.
- Send a note with a summary of the meeting and some useful piece of follow-up material or information for the buyer.
- Keep your main sponsor or contact in the loop regarding any meetings you have with his / her colleagues.

See also

Q15   How can I make a prospect's PA my sales ally?
Q17   How can we use LinkedIn for business development?
Q22   What preparation do we need to do before a sales meeting?
Q32   What should we do to make sure of a great sales presentation?
Q59   Why is selling to C-level executives different?

Q56   What should the business case look like?

Most sales proposals do not address the fundamental question every buyer needs answered — 'How is this purchase going to increase the performance of my business?'. Therefore, they don't provide the key information required in order to get a purchase approved – and so they don't get the sale.

Take, for example, the structure of the typical vendor proposal, compared to the structure of the buyer's business case or purchase approvals document:

Vendor's proposal	Buyer's business case
Problem	Strategic rationale – how the purchase fits with the goals and strategies of the business
Solution	Economic analysis — The costs / benefits of the purchase / chosen option
Benefits / features	Risk analysis – The project, technical, supplier and other risks involved
Cost	Recommendation – The recommended option to be pursued
Team, company and credentials	Implementation – The key success factors and implementation ingredients

Little wonder then that most sellers' proposals miss the mark.

See also

Q41   How can we help the buyer to buy?
Q46   How do we find out what buyers really want?

Q57 How do we differentiate ourselves from other suppliers?

According to buyers, most salespeople fail to communicate adequately the compelling reasons why buyers should buy their solutions.

Sellers who rely on benefits to sell are not telling buyers what they want to hear. As a result, they end up having the wrong conversations, at the wrong levels, with inevitable consequences on their sales success.

Benefits are rarely compelling. Most benefits are not worthy of discussion at the board table, because they rarely impact on the bottom line, at least not tangibly. They often are confused with features and with competitors. The opposite is true of business impact.

You must stop explaining why your solution is so great and instead show each buyer in turn how their business will be better as a result of implementing your solution. Back up your argument with real figures and real customer stories.

That's real differentiation!

See also

Q23 What are the top 15 customer questions and how should I handle them?

Q58   How do we manage the issue of risk for a buyer?

For buyers, this is the era of 'playing it safe'. The cost / benefits equation calculated in respect of each purchase has a vital new dimension – that of risk. Here are some of the implications for salespeople:

- You must be more sensitive to the issue of risk for the buyer. You must seek to minimise, or mitigate, it at every turn, through pilots, demos, phasing, third-party validation and reference sites.

- You need a sixth sense regarding buyer concerns, because they often go unstated. You must look out continuously for any signals that the buyer may be getting cold feet.

- Many risks arise because of misunderstanding, or lack of information. Tackle gaps in information or understanding – as these can lead to unnecessary concerns about risk.

- You must instil confidence – smaller vendors must make themselves look and, through alliances, act bigger.

- You must find ways to share the risk. In the past, the vendor disappeared after closing the sale, leaving the buyer 'holding the baby'. Payment tied to performance and other means of sharing risk are increasingly important today.

- Buyers often screen suppliers using criteria such as 'experience of our industry', 'relevant reference sites' etc. to minimise risk. You must address these factors up-front.

See also

Q49   How do we get a good understanding of what motivates the buying organisation and its key people?

Q80   Does the salesperson need to be involved after the sale has been won?

Q59   Why is selling to C-level executives different?

Increasingly, buying decisions are being made at higher levels. In these times of increased risk and uncertainty, senior managers personally are steering all significant purchase decisions.

But is selling to a CEO, or a CTO, different to selling to a mid-level manager? It sure is. Just as the view from the top floor of the company's offices is different to that at ground level, the agenda of the C-level executive is different to that of more junior management:

- They are focused on the strategic impact of any purchase on the performance of the organisation, taking a broader strategic view, focusing more clearly on issues of business performance, key business benefits and, of course, the business case.

- They are likely to be less interested in the detail – features and functions – and more concerned with business impact, levels of risk, return on investment, supplier credibility, etc.

- They may even use a different language – the language of strategy, business drivers, key performance indicators, return on investment, total cost of ownership, etc. They quickly bin traditional brochureware, looking instead for quantifiable results.

All these distinctions add further impetus to the move from selling products, technologies and features to selling solutions, their benefits and their business impact. To get attention at C-level, you need to be able to communicate quickly and compellingly how your solution can help achieve higher levels of performance in some key area of concern. You must back up that statement by citing other companies you have helped, telling stories of success and quantifying the benefits.

See also

Q52   Does one-to-one selling work?

SALES
ORDERS

Q60   How do we price our products / services?

Many sales managers struggle with the issue of price, since the ability to justify, negotiate and command high margins and prices is the supreme test of salesmanship, as well as the most meaningful measure of quality.

For economists, pricing is a relatively straightforward equation – that point where demand and supply meet. But, in the real world, pricing is much more complex. Even for rational buyers and economic buying decisions, price involves psychology and perception. Products and services that may be relatively similar in terms of form and function can be vastly different in price depending on brand name, styling and other quite subjective factors.

Here are some of the key questions sales managers should address in setting, or revising price:

- What is the cost? What do you need to charge to cover the cost of producing and delivering the product / service, as well as the cost of its development and marketing? Tips:
  - To avoid under-estimating the cost of marketing, take the cost of development and multiply it by 3.
  - Calculate the total cost of developing and taking your product / service to market, adding up all direct and indirect costs. Spread this over different estimates of volumes to be sold.
  - Add a profit margin, representing the return on investment and reward for risk to the promoters.
- What is the customer willing to pay? The answer to this question is based on an understanding of the value and the payback of your solution. What are the factors that determine the perceived value of the solution? Break your product / solution into components (scoping, pilot, installation, integration, commissioning, ongoing support, etc.) and, where possible, isolate the benefits / value associated with each. Re-arranging these components can impact on the value. Can you separate out different elements and charge for them individually? Tips:

- Keep in mind that price sensitivity, perceived need (or urgency) and value for money of your solution will vary greatly from segment to segment.
- These also will vary according to how you position your solution and the promises, benefits, or features that you highlight.

- How significant is the problem that the solution solves? What is the payback, or return on investment for the customer? What saving, or additional revenues will result from the solution? What is the customer's total cost of ownership? What proportion of that total cost does the initial price account for? Tips:
  - Create a spreadsheet to calculate the implication of your product / service on the customer's business.
  - Involve the customer in modelling the business case / return on investment for your solution. Be modest / realistic in your assumptions.
  - Track how customers apply and benefit from your solutions. Undertake a 'before and after' analysis of the impact.

- What are competitors charging? What do the alternatives cost? Tips:
  - Keep the list of alternatives as broad as possible, including the cost of alternative technologies or solutions and the cost of doing nothing.

See also

Q47   How do we establish the customer's buying criteria?
Q64   How do we manage a competitive bid?

Q61   Why should we give our prospects 'homework'?

After a successful meeting with a prospect, you leave full of enthusiasm and with a number of follow-up tasks to complete – for example, writing up and sending on a note of the meeting, forwarding a short technical brief (hopefully, template-based without too much customisation), offering a list of suggestions and next steps, perhaps even creating a summary proposal, or price quotation. All that may involve several hours work. Meanwhile, what does your prospect do? Well, probably nothing – which means that it could all have been a waste of time.

Selling requires the involvement of the buyer. Buyer and seller must move ahead in tandem, because it has to be a process of dual engagement and mutual commitment. So, there is no point in you, the salesperson, doing all the running, or taking on all the work.

To avoid this happening, you should build and test commitment incrementally – for example, by giving the buyer a test, in the form of some homework after a meeting, or a task to be completed prior to the preparation of a proposal. If the buyer does not complete the task successfully, then a red flag is raised regarding his / her level of commitment. This is an effective means of allowing the buyer to pre-qualify himself / herself by his / her own actions. This is important because words and deeds don't always match up. For example, the buyer may be saying the right things, but only because he / she is reluctant to say "No", even though there is no intention to buy.

So, for example, your prospect asks for a proposal after just one, or two, meetings. Rather than immediately saying "Yes", you might give the buyer a test by responding as follows: "Sure, I would be delighted to prepare a proposal for you, but in order for me to be able to do that effectively, would you ...?". The specific 'homework' might be:

- "Send me a one-page outline of your requirements, or a technical specification ...".

- "Introduce me to your colleagues in IT, so that I can check one or two pieces of information with them ...".

- "Send me a sample of the reporting provided by your existing system, so that I can understand the gaps as you have described them ...".

- "Give me a tour of the facility and allow me talk to some end-users ...".

The particular task should aim not only at testing, but also building, the buyer's commitment. If the buyer is prepared to take the time to prepare a specification, that is a sign that he / she is serious. The act of preparing the specification is a significant advance in the buying process, as well as an important input to enable you complete the next step of your sales process – in this example, the preparation of the proposal.

The principle of 'giving the prospect homework' is an important one. However, as with all techniques, it must be applied with care. Although it is a term that is in common usage, the language is a little off, particularly if you are a buyer. People don't like being told what to do and, just as in school days, most people don't like doing homework!

See also

Q36   How can we get the prospect to do our pre-qualification for us?

Q62   When should we walk away from a possible sale?

You cannot win them all – nor should you try. Sometimes, you should just walk away. It takes courage to say "No" to a request for a competitive tender. However, sometimes this is the wisest thing to do. Yet, many vendors automatically and instinctively jump at every opportunity. In particular, few companies have set criteria to determine when they will – and will not – tender. This means they are driven by how much they need or want a piece of work, as opposed to other considerations.

Pre-qualification takes place from day one. For example, if a company does not fit the criteria of a potential customer, they should not be on your target lists in the first place. Before putting pen to paper, make sure you are ready, willing and able to present a proposal, or make a quote.

A. Are you READY to propose?

- Has there been sufficient interaction with the buyer?
- Do you have the information we need?
- Have you established sufficient rapport among the buying unit?
- Has there been sufficient access to and engagement with the buying group (including stakeholders) to ensure they own the solution?
- Have solution scope and budget parameters been tested or agreed?

B. Are you WILLING to propose?

- Has the opportunity been reviewed internally?
- Is it business you want to go after?
- Are you prepared to invest the time?
- Will responding compromise other important sales activities?
- Do you believe you have a realistic chance of winning business now, or in the future, from this buyer?

- Has the opportunity been pre-qualified on budget, authority, timing and need?
- Is there an entrenched vendor?

C. Are you ABLE to propose?

- Can you put together a good proposal in the time required?
- Do you have enough information to do so?
- Do you fully understand the buyer's needs?
- Do you understand the essentials of the business case?
- Do you understand all the issues, constraints, nuances and risks?
- Do you have the solution they need?
- Do you have a relevant reference site / customer in their sector?

> **HINT**
>
> Pre-qualification takes place from the moment of first contact with a potential customer.

See also

Q40   What must we do to win the sale?
Q65   How can we boost win rates?

Q63   How can we make sure our sales proposal is focused on the buyer's needs?

From our experience of watching hundreds of sales presentations, pitches and proposals, we find that sellers spend nine times as much time on average talking about themselves (that is, their company and its solutions), as they do about the buyer's needs. It should be the other way around and, if it was, we believe it could double or triple the average salesperson's success rate.

So, how do you know where you, as a sales person, are focused? Listen to the words you use in sales pitches, presentations and proposals:

Focused on Needs Using these words suggests you are focused on the buyer's needs:	Focused Elsewhere Using these words suggests you are focused on your own solution:
Challenges / Needs	Competitive advantage
Problems / Opportunities	Benefits
Goals / Objectives	Features
Strategies	Technology
Priorities	Unique selling point
Performance gaps	Value proposition
Metrics	Our company, people, skills, capabilities, etc.
Results	Our services, products, or systems
Impact	'Industry-leading', 'best in class', 'innovative', etc.
Risk	Price

See also

Q32   What should we do to make sure of a great sales presentation?
Q62   When should we walk away from a possible sale?

Q64   How do we manage a competitive bid?

The growing popularity of competitive bids means sellers are losing control over how they sell. In many cases, they are reduced to selling by email, presentations and requests for proposals (RFPs). Although it is an unreliable and unpredictable means of selling, difficult market conditions mean vendors may not have a choice but to comply.

Use these tips to help you manage competitive bids:

- Decide when to bid and when not to bid: Many vendors automatically and instinctively respond to almost any request for a tender. That is because they don't have set criteria to determine when they will – and will not – tender. It takes courage to say "No" to a request for a competitive tender – especially when your order book is not over-full. However, sometimes this is the wisest thing to do. So, before putting pen to paper, make sure you are ready, willing and able to present a proposal to a new prospect.

- Set a budget for bidding: Just like any other area of sales and marketing, bid preparation should have a budget. Yet, few organisations set one, which is a mistake. As one sales manager put, it "Responding to requests for tenders that come in the post is a gamble, just like poker – if you don't decide what your limit is, you could lose your shirt!".

- Walk if you cannot talk: Unless the buyer is prepared to talk to you and to share sufficient information in advance of the RFx, then don't prepare a response. The result will be fewer, but better, RFxs – and likely more wins, too.

- Apply selling principles to the bid: Many buying teams adopt a hands-off approach to vendors in a competitive tender process and, as a result, many sellers have started to treat competitive bids very differently to other sales opportunities. However, your sales team must apply as much as possible of their normal sales tool kit to the competitive tender. That includes principles such as:
  - Nurturing the relationship in advance of any tender being published.

- Interacting with the buyer (within the constraints of the process) before submission and asking for the opportunity to interact again once submissions have been received.
- Researching the buyer's industry and business drivers.
- Looking behind the needs set out in the proposal to identify implicit needs.
- Quantifying impact and modelling benefits.
- Augmenting the requirements of the buyer and innovating in terms of the solution.

- Continuously improve bid quality: Many sellers admit to concerns around bid quality, not just the contents of the proposal, but how it is presented (including layout and proofing). This arises because bid preparation is often rushed, relies heavily on copying and pasting and does not get enough management time and input. Fewer but better proposals is a strategy that generally produces better results.

See also

Q65   How can we boost win rates?

An overall win rate is the sum of conversion rates at each stage of the sales process – from leads to sales meetings, from meetings to sales cycles, from cycles to orders and, finally, from initial orders to repeat customers. In other words, potentially everything that a salesperson does, and does not do, can impact on win rates.

Sales managers identify the top six priorities in boosting win rates as:

- Better quality sales leads (including pre-qualification and nurturing to sales-readiness).
- More effective sales meetings (with a multiple meeting approach and fewer presentations).
- More structured and systematic approaches to sales cycles (including building relationships, selling higher and wider, etc.).
- A gradual gaining of commitment in getting the order.
- Involving customers in proposal development to avoid 'surprises'.
- Moving from being a 'supplier' to a 'strategic partner'.

Sounds like a major challenge? A 3% increase in conversion rates at each of the stages above doubles the rate of sales growth in most organisations. We recommend starting with the easy areas to improve (for example, a new sales presenter, some sales training, a sales database, etc.) and continuous (if modest) improvements over time.

See also

Q13   What are the six challenges lead generation must overcome?
Q28   What can I do to make sales meetings more effective?
Q32   What should we do to make sure of a great sales presentation?
Q44   How can we shorten the sales cycle and accelerate the sale?
Q66   How can we improve the hit rate of our proposals?

Q66   How can we improve the hit rate of our proposals?

Salespeople write proposals assuming that they will be read and, if read, will be understood, appreciated, or even believed. Your proposal can't – and won't – sell for you, unless you have done all the groundwork first. As a general rule, the earlier a proposal is submitted, the lower the likelihood it will succeed. Also, the more proposals generated, the lower the likely overall rate of success. So, how do you ensure that, when you write a proposal, it has the maximum chance of success?

Here are some ways that salespeople we know increase their hit rates:

- Avoid pre-mature diagnosis by more systematic needs analysis.
- Avoid unilateral identification of needs and solutions – instead, use a bi-lateral approach, with lots of interaction, listening, probing, coaching, etc.
- Set clear criteria on when proposals will be prepared and when they will not.
- Involve the customer in writing the proposal, or write the proposal with the customer at your side.
- Avoid surprises – the role of the proposal is to confirm what has been already discussed, or agreed.
- Trial-balloon price and other aspects of the proposal and ensure you get feedback before a formal submission.
- Arrange a formal presentation of the proposal post-submission.
- Improve the quality and presentation of proposals, strengthening the customer references and the return on investment sections.

See also

Q67 How should we rate sales opportunities?

Almost every sales team has their own way of rating sales opportunities and, consequently, of arriving at a sales forecast. Yet, the accuracy of sales forecasts is rated as one of the key challenges faced by sales managers. How opportunities are rated requires more objectivity, consistency and science.

Too many sales managers are taken by surprise by stalled or lost buying decisions. That is because sales forecasts narrowly on the progress of the sales process, rather than on the buying process. For this reason, we analyse sales opportunities by asking three key questions:

1. Will they buy?
2. Will they buy now?
3. Will they buy from us?

Just because you are in pole position in terms of being the supplier of the choice (question 3 above) does not mean that you will win the sale. There are two other factors to be considered before you get to that point:

- Will they buy (for example, will the board sanction the purchase)?
- Will they buy now as opposed to later?

To address the first of these questions (will they buy?) requires a full understanding of the buying decision and, in particular, of the steps of the buying process, the requirements of the business case and the buy-in and support of the buying group. Today, organisations are faced with more projects competing for fewer resources and getting a purchase approved is increasingly demanding.

To address the second question (will they buy now?) requires answering such questions as:

- When will the buying decision be made?
- How important a priority is this?
- When will resources be allocated?
- What internal changes are required before commencement?

- How compelling and, indeed, time-dependent is the business decision? What is the cost of not acting now?
- Is there a triggering event, or driver for change?

The 'Will they buy from us?' question is more familiar territory for sellers analysing sales opportunities and, by and large, centres on whether your company is in pole position relative to competitors. Look at your relative competitive strength across both 'hard' and 'soft' dimensions. The 'hard' dimensions are how your proposal / solution measures up against the buying criteria; the 'soft' dimensions are such vital factors as the relationship, trust and interaction / engagement with the buyer.

See also

Q41 How can we help the buyer to buy?
Q48 What if the buying criteria set are not favourable to our company?
Q68 How do we spot opportunities that may be in trouble?
Q92 How can we be better at sales forecasting?

Q68 How do we spot opportunities that may be in trouble?

Based on a review of hundreds of pipeline opportunities, we have spotted some common early warning signals that an opportunity may be at risk. You know a sales opportunity is in trouble when:

- You don't have access to all the stakeholders.
- You don't have all the information needed.
- The same issues keep resurfacing repeatedly (covering old ground).
- You are doing all the running (buyer does not complete his actions).
- The buyer seems to be 'going along' with everything you say.
- Meetings are getting postponed or dates put back.
- Delays, setbacks or surprises are happening.
- You hear conflicting stories from within the buying organisation.
- There are sudden internal changes (people, priorities, mergers / acquisition, etc.)
- The buyer's industry or market is in a state of flux or turmoil.
- There are last-minute or rushed changes in requirements and specifications.
- Price issues arise too early (for example, before the requirements / scope has been set).
- The temperature of the relationship appears to have suddenly changed.
- There are political or personality issues in the buying organisation.
- Credibility questions are being asked continually about your company.
- You don't have a champion / coach in the buying organisation.

- You don't feel sufficiently respected (for example, the buyer always is late for meetings).
- Another supplier has a strong existing, or past, relationship with the buyer.
- Your gut instinct tells you something 'is off'.
- The business case is weak, absent, or kept from sight.
- There are competing projects vying for the same budget.

Use this list to review your top 10 sales opportunities for warning / danger signs.

See also

Q69 'Buyers only buy from big vendors'. What hope have we of selling to them?

According to professional buyers and some very successful salespeople, small to medium-sized companies (SMEs) have a huge problem selling to big companies. Why is this so and what needs to be done?

It's all about the language you speak
SME product and service providers don't face the same challenges their prospects face. One salesperson summed up the challenge well: "Working for a large organisation, we experience the same pressures as the people we sell to. We need to get a 2% to 3% cost reduction and to drive efficiencies, while ensuring customer value is maintained – and so do our customers. They know that and we know that. We speak the same language as the executives we meet (for example, capital costs, capex, opex, IRR), while most of the smaller specialist providers tends to focus on the benefits their offerings deliver".

Pack up your tent and go home or help the buyer buy?
The buyers and sellers we talk to suggest that the team targeting an executive in a major corporation needs to be clear that demand creation is their job. The executive won't say, "Here are my problems. Please help me solve them". In the current climate, big companies are looking to do more with less and the buyer will only work with a SME seller who can prove measurable impact quickly. As one buyer noted in a conversation with us recently, "The fact right now is big companies are not willing to take risk without an almost guaranteed payback and rock-solid business case. A small vendor who doesn't clearly present measurable benefits and an understanding of costs and risks will not succeed in this cautious environment".

Fear, uncertainty, doubt are centre-stage again
Big vendors are good at reducing fear, uncertainty and doubt and they will not be shy about raising the risk stakes if it means they can take a larger share of project-spend from a smaller provider.

But all is not lost – buyers like to buy from specialists
All of the above – size, trust, risk, the business case, the words you use – have implications for your route to market, the people who sell for you, how you target your message and, in many cases, the SME founders' willingness to develop partnerships with established players who can reduce risk in the eyes of the customer.

Some of our SME clients are selling successful to large organisations and their success seems to be based on their willingness to:

- Find the right solution for their customer.
- Align to their buyer's decision-making process.
- Learn how to speak their customer's language.
- Work with bigger partners who complement their offerings.
- Adopt a road-warrior mindset.

See also

Q11   How do we generate demand?
Q12   What are the 10 key steps in generating demand?
Q50   How can we change our language / approach to meet buyers' needs better?
Q58   How do we manage the issue of risk for a buyer?
Q64   How do we manage a competitive bid?

Q70 How do we know if the sale is ready to close?

Ultimately, the sale is ready to close only when the buyer is confident that he / she can get the purchase sanctioned. Because most managers no longer have the autonomy to make a major buying decision on their own authority, that means when:

- All the steps of the buying process have been concluded and the various requirements regarding procurement have been met, including the review points and hand-offs, and completion of the required information, analysis and documentation.

- The buyer has a compelling business case (including a full cost-benefit analysis, examination of risk and strategic fit, as well as implementation success) that justifies the purchase to whoever is required to sign it off.

- All those who needed to be consulted and involved have been addressed; the buying team has been fully involved, with the required consultation and buy-in achieved; and, in particular, the project has senior management support.

Thus the focus of your efforts in closing must be on ensuring that the buyer has everything that is required in order to make the decision, or to get the purchase sanctioned.

See also

Q71   What are the most effective closing techniques?

It may sound like a play on words, but the most effective closing techniques are those that help the buyer to buy. These techniques are the ones that help the buyer to build the business case, to ensure buy-in and to navigate the information and other requirements of their own organisation's buying process.

A major purchase is an important business decision, so the buyer won't be rushed into a premature decision. When everything is ready, the buyer will know how to close and will readily do so. Until the buying process has been navigated successfully, no closing technique will close the sale.

In particular, looking for a "Yes" on a proposal when there is a "No", or "Maybe" in terms of the business case is futile. In these cases, you must help the buyer make the business case more compelling if the project is to be approved.

As in all aspects of a complex sale, a consultative approach works best. So, your question is not "Are you ready to sign?" but "What do you want to do next?".

Use the following questions on the buyer to test whether the sale is ready to be closed:

- How close to completion is the business case?
- Do you believe the business case is compelling?
- Do you have all the information you need?
- Do you think there is anything missing?
- Do the numbers stack up?
- Do you think the issues of the various stakeholders have been adequately addressed?
- Is there anybody else that you need to meet?
- Are there any issues or concerns that remain unaddressed?

- How close to a decision do you think we are?
- What would you like to do next?
- Do you think the time is right to go for executive / board sign-off?
- Are you confident in predicting the way they will decide?
- Is there anything you think could cause a decision to be delayed?
- Are there any other events happening in the company that could impact on this?

See also

Q72   How can we increase our closing success?

Here are eight steps that can have a dramatic impact on your closing success:

- Business case, before sales proposal. Your sales proposal alone, no matter how good it is, won't get a major purchase sanctioned. Only a compelling business case can do that. So, you need to spend more time on the business case and less on the proposal.

- Proposals, without surprises. The only way to avoid surprises for both the buyer and seller is to ensure sufficient engagement prior to the preparation of any proposal. Proposals don't sell, or at least not very well. The golden rule is not to send a sales proposal when you should send a salesperson.

- Business impact, not benefits. Benefits don't mean a lot to buyers, because they don't relate to issues of interest to senior management. In short, benefits don't quantify the impact buying the solution will have on the business.

- Write the last page first. Sellers must write proposals the way buyers read them — that is, starting with the numbers. Rather than sheepishly delivering a price towards the back of a proposal document, you need to communicate a credible and compelling return on investment.

- Think risk and insurance. Risk is a part of the buying equation that sellers often overlook because it often goes unspoken. However, to attempt to close or negotiate when there are outstanding issues of risk is likely to result in failure. You need to create an environment of trust, where risks can be brought out into the open and dealt with.

- Walk if you cannot talk. There are some orders that you cannot win and, in these cases, it may make sense to cut your losses early. Having clear rules as to when you will, and will not, quote is vital.

- Close and negotiate with care. No aspect of selling is so dogged with misunderstanding than that of closing and negotiation. The result is the proliferation of out-dated closing and negotiation techniques that are completely at odds with the trust-based sale. Buyers no longer fall for the phony 'good cop – bad cop' or the 'closing room only' close. These techniques are likely to close the door, not the sale.

- Wish them well. If you don't win the sale (and you won't always), it is important to avoid the appearance of being a 'sore loser'. It is surprising how many deals fall through in the early stages, giving a second chance for the next in line. Maintaining a cordial relationship in spite of losing the deal can pay dividends at a later date.

These eight steps will enable you to carefully guide the sales opportunity through the often-tricky final steps of the sale. They bring to a successful conclusion all your efforts from the moment of inception of the lead, right through to the signing of the purchase order and they have a fundamental impact on win rates.

HINT

Close and negotiate with care.

See also

Q56   What should the business case look like?
Q58   How do we manage the issue of risk for a buyer?
Q62   When should we walk away from a possible sale?
Q65   How can we boost win rates?
Q66   How can we improve the hit rate of our proposals?
Q70   How do we know if the sale is ready to close?
Q71   What are the most effective closing techniques?
Q73   What should we do when we lose a sale?

Q73   What should we do when we lose a sale?

All salespeople become emotionally involved in winning the sale. It is not just a financial issue involving commissions and targets, but also an issue of personal pride: getting a "No" can feel like a slap in the face.

With this in mind, here are some tips on dealing with a lost sale:

- Don't blame yourself, or anybody else, and don't moan and complain either: focus instead on what can be learned from the situation.

- Don't personalise it: If you feel that you, or somebody else, 'dropped the ball', then focus your attention on the actions as opposed to the person. Focusing on behaviours, as opposed to people, is key to transforming destructive criticism into positive direction.

- Accept responsibility: Even if the market downturn, the departure of your key contact in the prospect company, the actions of a competitor, etc. have played a role in losing the sale, it is best not to focus on these things, but instead on how you and your company can / should deal with them. Accepting responsibility in this way is the key to leadership, to maintaining peace of mind and to moving forward.

- Learn from it: This transforms a set-back into an event that has the potential to improve your overall win rate. So, ask yourself (and all the others involved):
  - What will I / we do differently next time to get the result that I / we want?
  - Did I / we do everything possible? What worked? What would I / we not do again?

- Make the learning systematic, by undertaking win / loss analyses in respect of every proposal, or tender: That means asking questions such as:
  - Why did it come as such a big surprise? What clues did we miss?

- What was the gap between our solution and the prospect's perceived needs?
- Did we fully understand the needs?
- Did we ensure the prospect had all the information required?
- Did we clearly build trust and establish credibility?
- Did we identify and address all the barriers?
- Could we have made it any easier to say "Yes"?
- Did we invest enough time in building relationships?
- Did we cover the buying unit?
- Did we keep all our promises throughout?
- Were there any aspects of how we managed the sales cycle that could have been improved?

- Ask for feedback and advice from the prospect who has just said "No": Make it easy for the people involved to open up and tell you the real reasons. Take great care not to appear as a 'sore loser'. Swallow your pride and genuinely wish them the best in implementing their chosen solution.

- Stay positive: See the setback as an opportunity to grow, improve and become stronger. You may have lost this sale, but that does not mean that you have lost the potential customer. It is important to keep in touch with the customer, even though they have chosen another supplier. Things change and suppliers, as well as managers, come and go – if you maintain the relationship, you may find yourself in pole position for the next order.

See also

Q67 How should we rate sales opportunities?
Q72 How can we increase our closing success?
Q76 Why are customers lost?

Q74   What do we do when a client wants to re-negotiate on price?

Most buyers are passing on the pain of budget cuts to their suppliers, who have no choice in the present sales climate but to grin and bear it.

However, some suppliers are better insulated against cuts than others, specifically those with whom relationships are strongest, satisfaction is highest and, most important of all, those who are able to quantify their impact on key business drivers. Another group faring better than average is suppliers who have adopted a pro-active approach – dealing with the issue of pricing before they receive an email or phone call from the purchasing department.

Here are some tips on how to deal with a request for reduced pricing from a customer. Ask the hard questions first:

- Is the contract worth it? Will your company die without this contract? What is the balance of power? Is the customer a good payer? How profitable is the work?

- What are the buyer's motivations? What are the underlying business drivers for the customer? Is it cutting costs, driving efficiencies, minding cash, targeting non-essential costs, delaying capital projects, or maximising revenue / value capture? Which of these is involved can have a subtle, but important, impact on how to re-negotiate price.

- How valuable is the relationship? How successful the re-negotiation is depends on the relationship in question. How far you are prepared to go to meet the customer's needs depends on how important the customer is to your business.

- What is the bottom-line impact? Go back to your project budget, your cash flow and your P&L. What impact will price cuts have? What is the impact on margins and profits of different strategies to achieve cuts of 5%, 10% and 15%? Some aspects of projects are less profitable than others, some may even be sub-contracted and deliver only small margins – target these areas for greatest cuts.

- What is the market outlook? What are competitors charging? What is the cost of switching?

Strategies to use in re-negotiation:

- Prepare for the negotiation: Practise lots of scenarios – ensure you have competitor pricing, use information from project reviews, come with suggestions, play 'good cop – bad cop', don't decide there and then but allow time to consider.

- Revisit your contract: What does your contract stipulate in terms of re-negotiation? Although you may adhere to requests for re-negotiation, even if not technically required under contract, timing and related issues are very important. 'All deals are re-negotiable', but that largely depends on the bargaining power of the parties involved.

- Use the right people to re-negotiate: The choice of who sits in on the re-negotiation is very important. Don't just leave it to the person who is dealing with the account on a day-to-day basis. Ensure any re-negotiation is submitted for approval to the most senior level.

- Decide in advance your final negotiating position and how you are going to try to improve on it. Consider the milestones in the negotiation from your buyer's perspective.

- What is the *quid pro quo*? With a win-win in mind, what can the buyer offer in return for a price cut? For example, "If you're unhappy with the price we've agreed and want it cheaper, then I might be willing to re-negotiate in return for a higher volume of orders from you".

Key principles to follow include:

- Adopt a win-win approach: Handle it well – put yourself in the buyer's shoes – it is not personal, it's business. Once the issue of a re-negotiation is raised, deal with it pro-actively, and put a process and timeline in place to address the issue.

- Pass on your savings immediately, and if you don't have any to pass on, start cutting your costs and re-negotiating with your own suppliers.

- Reframe the issues in terms of value, or the impact of your solution / services on the customer's business. Have the anticipated benefits been achieved? Have unanticipated benefits arisen? Now that you know the client, the environment, etc. much better than you did when the project began, or when you crafted the proposal, you can bring that learning to bear on the project and cost benefit review with the purchasing / procurement officer.

- Focus on efficiencies and driving additional benefits / value: Quantify the impact your solution has in the customer's business and identify ways in which this can be maximised. It may seem like you are revisiting some of the earlier stages of the sales process, but re-affirming needs and payback for the customer is important.

- Examine the total cost of the solution: Your cost may only be a small proportion of the total cost to the customer. For example, a software client's price was €1.5 million; however, the customer organisation had allocated 50 IT staff for 12 months to the implementation project, which more than doubled the budget. Targeting this area could identify a wide range of savings.

Find innovative ways to cut the cost:

- Price differentiation: Identify changes in the product / service that can have a significant impact on perceived value – for example, support levels, feature set, scalability, etc. – which may cost very little, but greatly impact on the level of perceived value.

- Simplify the product: Sometimes you have to stop adding value, when it adds too much to your product cost.

- Re-package and re-bundle: Break your solution down into components of value and cost. For example:
    - Target reductions in support costs – for example, improved self-service help functionality, or remote monitoring.
    - More flexible pricing (for example, software as a service) or delivery models (for example, phased implementations).

- Offer self-provisioning / internal fulfilment of parts of the solution – for example, the customer provides manpower resources to reduce the implementation budget.

HINT

How far you are prepared to go to meet a customer's need depends on how important the customer is to your business.

See also

Q49 How do we get a good understanding of what motivates the buying organisation and its key people?

Q57 How do we differentiate ourselves from other suppliers?

Q60 How do we price our products / services?

REPEAT
SALES

Q75   Why are pilots risky for sellers?

Pilots play an increasingly important role in the sales process. They are not the fastest way to secure a sale but, in a high-risk business climate, they can provide a vehicle to make tangible product benefits and, thereby, to secure buyer commitment.

The reality, however, is that, while pilots reduce the risk for the buyer, they can have the opposite effect for the seller. Pilots can be expensive, they elongate the sales cycle and, if problematic, they can be very difficult to recover from. For early-stage companies, this is all the more important, since successful pilots are important in providing third-party product validation and customer reference sites for future marketing.

So, why do many pilots fail? Here are the top five reasons:

- The pilot is entered into too readily, by the buyer or the salesperson. In particular, this can happen with complex pilots that require a significant commitment of time and resources on either part.

- The pilot showcases the technology, but fails to prove the business case. While IT managers, for example, are delighted with the technology, that enthusiasm does not translate into a valid business case at C-level.

- Clear and realistic success criteria are not agreed, resulting in a mismatch of expectations, and the lack of a process for moving the buying decision forward post-trial. In too many cases, customer criteria for evaluating pilot success are not written down and reviewed against results. For the selling organisation, there is often limited contact with end-users and, consequently, the lack of real feedback from the 'coal-face'.

- Poor implementation on either side: poor client-side implementation, often stemming from a 'not invented here' mentality on the part of whoever has been delegated to manage the pilot; and failure by the selling organisation to manage the pilot and, in particular, how the solution is used to avoid surprises, or problems, during implementation.

- Priorities in the company change, or perhaps people, or politics change – the longer the pilot, the greater the risk here.

HINT

Pilots can be expensive, they elongate the sales cycle and, if problematic, can be very difficult to recover from.

See also

Q58 How do we manage the issue of risk for a buyer?
Q59 Why is selling to C-level executives different?

Q76   Why are customers lost?

The first sale to a customer involves making promises, while the repeat sale requires you to keep those promises. This is at the core of why many customers are lost. Promises made and expectations set during the sale have not been met – and so the customer does not trust or believe you sufficiently to buy again.

Customers are lost when the promise is greater than the product or the performance. There are lots of words to describe when this happens:

- Product quality.
- Service quality.
- Delivery problems.
- Poor customer service / after-sales support.
- Poor account management.
- Poor communication.
- Project management failures.

As a seller, you must manage the expectations, manage the performance and continually communicate the benefits achieved by customers post-sale.

As far as buyers are concerned, most suppliers are expendable. This is a real problem in tough markets where there are many suppliers chasing few customers. Your customers are at risk of being lured by the competing promises of other vendors. So, even keeping the promises you made last quarter or last year may not be enough. It is vital that you are pro-active, rather than re-active in terms of meeting the changing needs of your key customers.

See also

Q73   What should we do when we lose a sale?
Q79   What are the main barriers to repeat sales?
Q83   How do we ensure customer loyalty?

Q77   How can we maximise customer referrals?

This checklist will help you to maximise sales referrals for your business:

- Analyse the source of your sales: Check to see where your sales, leads and enquiries come from and the closure rates for each source. How many are derived from customer referrals?

- Set a target for referrals: How many of your customers have you asked for a referral in the past year? Set a target for the number of referrals you want to get over the next year and the value of additional sales you expect as a result.

- Put a plan in place for referral-generated sales: Don't leave referrals to chance – list all the actions required by sales and service to meet your sales referral targets. Put names, as well as completion and review dates, beside all those from whom referrals are to be sought.

- Make sales referrals a part of your key account management plans: When your team is discussing key customer accounts, put sales referrals on the agenda.

- Deliver on your promises: If you want referrals, then you must deliver on your promises first, ensuring that your customer is satisfied with your product and service. Before you ask for a referral, ask the customer for feedback. This will identify either opportunities for strengthening your relationship with your customer, or pave the way for referrals, or testimonials.

- Be an expert, not a sales person: If your customer considers you to be an expert, a solutions provider, or a problem-solver, as opposed to a salesperson, then you have made it easy for him / her to pass on a referral. After all, everybody is cautious about setting a salesperson loose on a friend, or colleague.

- Become a partner, not a supplier: If you are a problem-solver, as opposed to a sales-person, then to be consistent your organisation should position itself as a partner, not just a supplier. It's a small change in terminology, but a major difference in mindset and one that your customer will reward you for.

- Share sales commissions on referral business with service and support staff: Referral business comes from good service, as much as good salesmanship, so it makes sense to reward and encourage service staff for sales referrals.

- Make your buyer and his / her manager look good: When a buyer or manager in a customer organisation passes on referrals, in effect they are saying a personal "Thank you". One simple way to repay them is to make them look good by providing them with specialist training, information and ideas of help to them.

- Ask, but at the right time: Don't ask for referrals before it is reasonable to do so. Wait until the customer has experienced your company and its products sufficiently to be able to pass judgement, both for themselves and others. It is unfair to ask the customer to attach his good name to something that he / she has had only limited experience of. More important, it makes you look pushy if you ask for a referral the minute you have closed the sale.

- Ask, but only the right people: Make a list of the customers you can ask for referrals. Not all customers will be raving fans of your company; perhaps another contact in the same company may be more positively disposed to helping you.

- Ask your customers for testimonials and agree where they can be used: What your customers say about you, particularly where they attach their name to it, has more impact that anything you, or your marketing people, have to say. Use it wisely – and only with their permission.

- Generate publicity for your customer (and yourself): Another important way to benefit from what you have done for your customer and to generate referral business is to get publicity for your clients. For example, if your customer has just implemented your technology, help them to get trade press publicity regarding their new capabilities and facilities.

- Say "Thank you" for referrals: Make a point of calling your customer to say "Thank you" and of updating your customer on how things progress with the referral. Find another way of showing your gratitude if your customer's company policy dictates against gifts.

- Provide an incentive for referrals (if appropriate): Any ongoing arrangement regarding referrals should involve a referral fee, or a percentage based on resulting sales. In settling on this percentage, it is useful to analyse the relative cost of generating a sales lead and closing a sale (from different sources).

- Pass referrals both ways: One of the best ways to encourage referrals is to provide your customer, or partner with referrals / useful contacts in turn.

- Use LinkedIn to ask for referrals from your contacts: Look at who your contacts know and ask for an introduction to those who may represent potential customers.

HINT

When getting publicity for customers, let them take most of the credit, as long as your company's name and its products are mentioned.

See also

Q78　We have won the order. The selling is over, right?

Wrong, you have only reached the end of round one. Since you probably need to win the customer's future business and recommendation, not just this order, there's lots more work to do.

Too many suppliers install their solutions and then collect the annual maintenance and support, but forget to measure the impact that their solutions have on their customers. For some, there is a fear that the results shown will be disappointing; for others, there is the lack of a methodology, model or formula for calculating the results. Bottom line, they lack the ability to guide their customers through a before-and-after analysis of the success of their solution.

Quantifiable information about the impact of your solution is not just nice to have, it is essential. It not only enables you to demonstrate the impact on your solution on your customer's business, but provides you with the confidence to build a compelling business case for your other prospects.

So, here is a checklist:

- Do you have a model to calculate the impact of your solution and to demonstrate the business case?
- If so, what are the top metrics used by customers to assess the impact of your solution?
- Do you have before-and-after information for your customer?
- Does the customer believe the performance and impact metrics you produce? Is he / she involved in the process of their preparation?
- Are key business impact and solution performance metrics discussed at client-side meetings / reviews?
- Are senior management in the client company aware of the impact of your solution?
- Is first-hand user feedback incorporated into product and innovation management processes in your company?

HINT

Quantifiable information about the impact of your solution is essential to build a compelling business case for other prospects.

See also

Q76 Why are customers lost?
Q80 Does the salesperson need to be involved after the sale has been won?

Q79   What are the main barriers to repeat sales?

Ensuring repeat sales and developing a long-term relationship with clients revolves around one simple but rarely completed equation:

Promise = Performance.

While getting the first sale involves making promises, securing the second sale requires keeping them. Salespeople often feel they will lose a sale if they don't promise enough, but often lose out on subsequent sales by promising too much.

The ultimate measure of success for any organisation is its ability to develop long-term customer relationships and, thus, repeat business. High rates of growth and profitability are unsustainable unless organisations can apply the same sophistication and skill to keeping existing customers as they do to finding new ones. But the ability to nurture clients and grow existing business is one of the biggest failings of most sellers, even though it requires half the salespeople, half the sales calls and half the proposals.

The equation *Promise = Performance* not only focuses organisations on delivering results and generating repeat sales, it also enables them to seek referrals from clients — one of the most effective ways to generate leads but also one of the most under-used.

To meet a repeat sales target, redirect your efforts from helping the customer to buy, to helping the customer succeed. Thus, your role as a salesperson changes from making promises to keeping promises. While this might sound easy, organisations are often complacent when it comes to their existing client-base. Research highlights that only one-quarter of promises made by vendors are kept; as a result, one-in-five managers are willing to consider changing from their existing supplier.

See also

Q77   How can we maximise customer referrals?
Q89   Why are referrals so important?

Q80   Does the salesperson need to be involved after the sale has been won?

With lengthening sales cycles, you are likely to be under pressure once the deal has been signed to move on to close the next opportunity. However, the danger is that you do so at a time when buyer anticipation and anxiety is at its greatest.

Buyers often complain the attention, enthusiasm and commitment shown by sellers during the sales process wanes (often dramatically) once the order is signed. Instead of the seller chasing the buyer, the situation is reversed. This happens all too often when the salesperson fails to pass the baton successfully to their support / service colleagues.

Just when you think your job as salesperson is done, another vital phase of the sales process is about to begin — implementation. So it makes sense that the lead salespeople handhold and support the customer at the early stages of a project.

You should never shirk the responsibility of ensuring project success, although it is essential that you hand over the day-to-day project management and delivery to the experts. Buyer confidence depends on a smooth transition, so it is crucial that the person who takes over the day-to-day management of the project has been involved during the sales process. It is also really important for the salesperson to maintain contact with their delivery team and the buyer's implementation team. Salespeople cement and deepen the relationship by staying in touch after the sale.

See also

Q78   We have won the order. The selling is over, right?
Q85   What are the key elements of account management?

Q81   How do we increase our importance to the customer?

Many companies make bold promises about their commitment to customer service: 'High performance guaranteed', 'It's all about customer service', etc. However, independent vendor research at the height of the boom put customer disaffection at 25%+. Clearly, customer service is more than a slogan.

Here is the test: Do your customers see your company as being genuinely and passionately committed to *their* success? The answer to this question is perhaps the ultimate measure of your company's ability to sell more to its existing customers.

Unless you continuously add value, develop the relationship and, for example, innovate in terms of delivery, then your client is vulnerable to being poached by a competitor.

From the customer's perspective, it is your organisation's performance last week and last month, not last year or the year before, that matters.

Suppliers cannot live long on their laurels, hence the importance of ongoing innovation and improvement. To be secure, you must anticipate your customer's present and future needs and engage in an ongoing dialogue about these needs. You must demonstrate not only your organisation's capability to deliver, but also a genuine commitment to the buyer's success.

Key elements of building such a strategic relationship are when:

- You contribute to the achievement of an important customer objective or strategy in a manner that is visible, quantifiable and direct.
- You have access to the buyer's boardroom and are considered a trusted advisor.
- The customer calls on your expertise.

- Your products and skills are considered to be specific or, at least, tailored to the unique requirements of the customer and its industry.
- You go beyond meeting the customer's present needs by anticipating future needs.
- You go beyond merely providing products and services to the client, and focus your resources on impacting on the customer's business.
- You 'blur the lines' between the customer and supplier relationship by:
  - Sharing people, ideas, technologies and so on.
  - Inspiring the buyer, through innovation and leadership.
  - Involving customers in product / process development.
  - Integrating processes, systems, supply chains and shared assets.
  - Sharing the risk and the reward, including new commercial models.

See also

Q76   Why are customers lost?
Q79   What are the main barriers to repeat sales?
Q82   How do we communicate our importance to the customer?
Q87   How can we protect our customers from hungry competitors?

Q82   How do we communicate our importance to the customer?

There must be a visible link between your solutions and your customer's success. However, you cannot assume that customers fully appreciate the value you add or the impact you have on their business. So, as a supplier, it's your job to make sure this is very clear.

As customer success is your goal as a salesperson, and business impact is the measure of that success, then the formula by which it will be measured and the process by which it is to be documented are vital. In particular, both buyer and seller should be focused on the key metrics (cost savings generated, time to market, etc.) by which success will be tracked. Customers can quickly take suppliers and their solutions for granted, it is the seller's job to ensure that this does not happen.

In short, the job of the sales and delivery organisation is to document and discuss success right throughout the customer relationship. To sell more, you need to reinforce success more, continually reminding the seller of the benefits gained and promises met.

HINT	Both buyer and seller should be focused on the key metrics by which success will be tracked.

See also

Q81   How do we increase our importance to the customer?

Q83   How do we ensure customer loyalty?

Getting the first sale requires helping the customer to buy. However, ensuring you get the second (and subsequent) sale comes down to your ability to contribute to your customer's success.

Sales managers often ask '"How can we take more revenue from that account?". However, suppliers need to change the focus to "How can we help the customer more?". Growing revenue from existing customers requires identifying not just opportunities to up-sell and cross-sell, but also opportunities to contribute more tangibly to the customer's success.

To meet your target, you must help the customer meet their target too. So, rather than looking simply to take an even larger share of the buyer's limited budget, you should look for new ways to:

- Make the buyer's budget go further.
- Help the buyer do more for less.
- Accelerate the buyer's progress towards their goals.

All of these will help the buyer to meet his / her targets, will build a trusting relationship and, over time, will lead to repeat sales.

See also

Q81   How do we increase our importance to the customer?
Q84   How do we become more pro-active in managing customer
       relationships?

Q84   How do we become more pro-active in managing customer relationships?

Most managers suggest they are 'not as pro-active as they should be' when it comes to customer relationships. As a result, they are often caught off guard when:

- A change in personnel in the customer's organisation occurs.
- A new supplier appears.
- Negative customer feedback is received.
- Delivery or quality problems occur.
- Contracts are put out to tender with no advance notice.
- Business priorities and strategies change that have a knock-on effect on terms.

The sad reality is that, in many organisations, customer retention, customer loyalty and customer satisfaction are mere buzzwords. They are not measured or managed, and do not get enough time and attention from sales, operations and the executive management team.

Sellers must become more pro-active, pre-empting customer needs and innovating constantly in terms of their solutions. That includes:

- Pre-empting problems the customer may have.
- Reviewing quality levels with the customer and how they can be improved.
- Looking beyond the scope of its current project to the impact on other areas of the customer's business.
- Anticipating possible future needs of the customer.
- Sharing new ideas and opportunities for innovation or improvement.
- Holding follow-up reviews to understand how the solution is being used and how results can be maximised.

- Identifying how the total cost of its solutions can be minimised for the customer by eliminating or overhauling inefficient processes.
- Providing follow-up training courses to ensure widespread system adoption of the chosen solution.

See also

Q83   How do we ensure customer loyalty?

Q85   What are the key elements of account management?

The key activities associated with account management are listed below. Are they being undertaken in your organisation?

- Sales and profitability analysis: Classifying accounts based on revenue, profit performance and potential by employing activity-based accounting methods.
- Client feedback: Gathering feedback from clients in a formal, systematic and documented manner.
- Internal reviews: Bringing together the project team for each account to review performance, opportunities and actions.
- Client-side reviews: Undertaking reviews with clients at their premises to assess performance, identify any issues and understand changing priorities and directions.
- Categorisation of accounts: Categorising accounts on their performance and potential.
- Policies / Targets: Setting targets regarding service levels, responsiveness and performance for each customer category.
- Key account plans: Developing a plan for each key account that sets out how to grow account revenue and profitability, as well as how to deepen the client relationship, and deliver greater value and service.
- Revenue and profitability targets: Setting and revising targets for revenue, as well as profits from existing customers and innovations in service / delivery to increase customer value.
- CRM system: Using a CRM system or sales database to store customer data and manage customer relationships effectively.

See also

Q86   What is the difference between account management and account development?

Q86 What is the difference between account management and account development?

The main difference between account management and account development is the focus on client success. So, the right question is not "How are we managing the account?" but "How are we helping the customer to succeed?".

Account development is a long-term proposition and views relationships as more than the sum of individual contracts or projects. It is where the seller believes 'we can be good together' and demonstrates to the buyer that they want to contribute further to the buyer's success. In key accounts, the supplier strives to be more than just a supplier — the aim is to become a strategic partner.

In order to make good on this promise, you need to understand the evolving dynamics of the buyer's business and to connect with the buyer's strategic objectives. You must invest in building the relationship post-sale, seeking to ensure your contact base is higher, wider and deeper within the customer's organisation.

Innovation is one of the most important characteristics of this special type of relationship and is reflected in the two-way exchange of ideas between supplier and customer.

See also

Q83 How do we ensure customer loyalty?
Q84 How do we become more pro-active in managing customer relationships?
Q85 What are the key elements of account management?

Q87   How can we protect our customers from hungry competitors?

After a decade of buoyant demand, organisations face a battle on two fronts – to protect existing customer revenues from being poached by competitors, while seeking out any new business that exists in the marketplace.

Salespeople increasingly are wandering into new territories in search of whatever business is to be found. In fact, one buyer told us recently that he was now receiving half-a-dozen sales calls each day, the majority of which were from suppliers that had never previously contacted his company. So it is no wonder that sales managers are complaining about new competitors circulating around their hard-won customers, luring them with discounted prices. For buyers facing mounting cost pressure, the temptation can be just too great to resist.

Here are some strategies that you can use to protect your customers from increased competition:

- Stop managing key accounts, develop them instead: Your relationship with a customer cannot remain static, in spite of changes in personnel, budgets, competition, business priorities, and so on. You have to keep moving along those accounts that are important – pro-actively nurturing and growing them – recognising that the sales job is not over when the order is won.

- Understand and reflect changing buying priorities: Your customer's business and its priorities are radically different to what they were six or 12 months ago. Their focus is likely to be more short-term, and they are likely to be looking to adopt a leaner, more flexible and more innovative approach to all aspects of their business. It is important that the way your company does business reflects these changes.

- Help your customer through the downturn: Almost universally, customers are facing tighter budgets, pressure on costs and demands for increased efficiency. As a supplier, how can your services and solutions aid the customer in these areas? Use your understanding of the extent of user adoption, the impact on related business processes, underused system functionality, etc. to show your customer how to squeeze further efficiencies and costs.

- Communicate the value: Your customer is rightly asking "What have you done for me lately?", thus it is vitally important to measure the impact of your solution on the customer's business.

- Innovate continuously: Because your competitors are likely to be approaching your customers promising something different, it is important that you also continuously innovate and differentiate in terms of what you are providing.

- Don't settle for just being a supplier: For customers that are strategically important to your business, you must work to deepen the relationship and move along the continuum from supplier to strategic partner, which will require greater levels of mutual communication, interaction, understanding and trust.

- Make switching more difficult: Seek to make your customer more dependent on you, or to tie them to your solution by means of your terms, the proprietary nature of the technology employed, the level of integration of your solution with the customer's other systems, or processes, or simply great service and strong relationships.

- Be pro-active: Plan ahead with your key accounts – for example, pre-empt price renegotiations, changes in the customer's strategy, or personnel, etc. Too often, suppliers are taken off guard by changes in a customer's business, or requirements.

See also

Q88   How should we measure customer satisfaction?

You probably believe that customer satisfaction is very important. However, it is becoming increasingly clear that it is not. The problem is that what customers say and how they act with customer satisfaction surveys (although important) is a poor predictor of buying behaviour or customer loyalty.

So, the pursuit of customer satisfaction as the end goal of sales and marketing is misguided. Satisfaction is a fluffy and woolly concept that misses the whole point of the buyer-seller relationship. It is not the satisfaction of the buyer that matters, but the results you have helped them achieve.

Asking your clients whether they are satisfied is simply the wrong question. Sellers must measure themselves on the metrics used by their customers. So, instead of saying 67% of our customers are satisfied or very satisfied, you should be able to say something like:

- "75% of our customers saved more than they expected using our solutions, with the average saving equating to 5% of total project costs".

- "1.25% was the improvement of margins resulting from the implementation of our solutions".

- "Our customers have improved stock accuracy levels by 20% since the implementation of our solutions, with the net bottom line impact of 2%".

See also

Q83   How do we ensure customer loyalty?
Q87   How can we protect our customers from hungry competitors?

Q89 Why are referrals so important?

We all use the advice of friends and colleagues, as well as of experts, to guide our buying decisions. We are happy to recommend those from whom we have received good service. However, we are rarely asked to do so. It follows that one of the most effective and immediate ways to boost your sales pipeline and, ultimately, your sales is to ask customers for referrals. Yet it is so often over-looked, with only a minority of salespeople actively using customer referrals to sell.

Existing and past customers can spread the good word about your business more convincingly than any ads or brochures. Indeed, the closure rate from customer referrals is likely to be two or three times that of your normal sales leads.

In addition to higher win rates, referrals result in faster sales cycles. When you are introduced or referred, then you are marked aside from the traditional salesperson, you gain a badge of trust and credibility that can move you to the inner circle and ensure that you are treated as an expert and a problem-solver, not as a salesperson.

More effective than any glossy marketing brochures are letters of recommendation from customers. They are more believable, more interesting and more memorable. They mean that cynical buyers don't have to take your word for it, since you provide third-party validation and peer references or social proof.

No salesperson on your team should visit customers without having a selection of letters from customers saying how they have benefited from the products or services that were supplied by your organisation.

The most effective sales presentations replace long lists of features and benefits with stories of how other companies have benefited from their solutions. They replace technical information that is only of interest / accessible to a select few, with details of how their solutions have impacted on key business opportunities, challenges and metrics.

See also

Q77   How can we maximise customer referrals?

SALES MANAGEMENT

Q90   Who do we need on our selling team?

Gone are the days a solo salesperson could sell high value deals without help from domain, technology and delivery experts – which has implications for the sales and relationship competencies across your organisation.

In a sales team, there are a number of key roles critical to moving opportunities from leads to meetings to sales cycles to orders:

- A sales person, who adopts an expert-led and consultative selling approach.
- A pre-sales support person, who knows the domain.
- A product / market expert, who can talk knowledgeably about the industry.
- A product director, who owns the technology vision and road map.
- A senior developer, who can be paired off with senior tech staff from the client / buying team.
- An account manager, who can be introduced towards the end of the sales cycle, who has delivered similar projects previously.
- An implementation / customer services driver, who will manage delivery, customer service and steering group reviews.
- The MD, and maybe even the chairman, to build confidence and add gravitas.

In the most successful organisations, sales is everybody's job and everyone is on the team.

See also

Q98   How can we improve our recruitment of sales staff?

Q91 What are the obstacles that prevent individual salespeople selling more?

What is getting in the way of each of your salespeople selling more?

Many managers are afraid to ask this question, fearing the result will be a list of excuses. However, once potential barriers (real or imagined) are clearly identified, they can be tackled head on. The most common are:

- The relationship with the manager.
- Levels of marketing and support.
- Changes in the market (for example, competition).
- The sales message or proposition.
- Inefficient sales systems.

Here are key areas in which salespeople can be helped to sell more:

- Leadership: Including building trust and respect, better communication, involvement in decisions, leading by example, clarity of responsibilities and direction, consistency, etc.
- Support: Assistance in the following areas:
  - Messaging (how to communicate a compelling proposition for the customer).
  - Marketing support / materials / sales aids / building awareness / references.
  - Product / industry knowledge and market intelligence (including competitor analysis, etc.).
  - Sales training and coaching.
  - Pre-sales support.
  - Delivery / implementation / customer service / account management / support.
  - Ensuring sales targets are realistic.
- More time for selling: Reduce time spent on lead generation, sales reporting, admin, preparing proposals, travelling and other non-sales areas (for example, product meetings, order fulfilment, etc.).

- More and better leads:
    - Assist the salesperson to be more effective in generating more of his / her own leads (buying, or building lists, direct mail shots, marketing support, etc.).
    - Provide the salesperson with more and better leads in order to support his / her own lead generation, contacts, black-book, introductions, etc.
- Sales systems: The effective use of a good sales system allows sales people to reduce reporting time, improve levels of personal organisation and increase sales effectiveness (conversion rates). Yet most sales people regularly complain that sales databases are cumbersome, slow, lacking in functionality and contain out-of-date information. You may need to:
    - Upgrade or replace your system to ensure full usability and functionality.
    - Provide more training and user support.
    - Provide administrative support (including purging the system of redundant information, etc.).
    - Make use of the system compulsory (linking it to payment of commissions, etc.).
- Strategic issues, dealing with the following objections:
    - Competitive advantage (from pricing to product comparison).
    - The marketplace is in a state of change.
    - We are not well-known in the marketplace.
    - We need to build our brand, or change our reputation.
    - We need more / better reference sites / customers.
    - We need to re-examine the markets we are serving (geographic, sectoral, etc.).

See also

Q23   What are the top 15 customer questions and how should I handle them?

Q100 How can we increase the effectiveness of our sales team?

Q92   How can we be better at sales forecasting?

Successful sales forecast accuracy and sales reporting have at their core:

- Visibility of what is happening year to date (that is, historical sales activity levels, sales revenue and margins).

- Predictability of what is going to happen to the year-end and thereafter (including booked and forecast sales, required activity levels and conversion rates).

- Control (that is, the ability to impact on the level and effectiveness of sales activity, thereby immediately correcting any gaps and continually optimising people and process performance).

Greater visibility comes at a price. It generally requires:

- Better systems: Implementation of reporting systems, stricter forecasting methods, and even sales database or CRM systems.

- Better structures: A more structured approach to sales meetings, sales reporting and customer reviews.

- Better plans: And, more importantly, an approach to planning and target-setting that sets out targets and metrics, not just based on sales, but on levels of activity (for example, number of sales meetings required) and effectiveness (that is, conversion rates throughout the sales cycle and, ultimately, win rates).

- Better processes: A more structured approach to the management of sales cycles, to enable more accurate pipeline forecasts and the rating of individual sales opportunities.

It is important that sales managers move from subjective measures to ratings based on the completion of specific elements of the sales process (for example, documentation of needs analysis, contact with all members of the buying unit, or presentation of ROI models).

See also

Q7   Is there a better way to forecast sales than relying on market
        research?
Q67   How should we rate sales opportunities?
Q93   Why do we need a sales system?

Q93   Why do we need a sales system?

Imagine an accountant without an accounts package, or an architect without a CAD programme! Well, most sales organisations do not have a widely-used and effective sales system, which costs them dearly in terms of lost sales, as well as lost time and effort.

Here are 12 compelling reasons why you need a good sales system:

- It increases conversion rates at all stages of the sales cycle. A sales system enables sales opportunities and leads to be managed more effectively, especially through the universal application of a more consistent and effective sales process.

- It enables a more systematic, structured and managed approach to the management of sales; leads, opportunities, etc. Nothing is left to chance as salespeople and their managers easily can identify neglected accounts, leads that need to be followed up and opportunities that require more work before closing.

- It provides increased visibility, predictability and control in respect of sales. That means managers can see what is happening; they can use this information to predict what is going to happen (using inbuilt forecasting tools) and can take action, without waiting for the quarter's results or the next sales meeting.

- It provides more accurate and reliable sales pipeline forecasts. More information is available and is more up-to-date. Also, a sales system tempers salespeople's natural optimism by providing a common sales language (when is a hot prospect 'hot'?) and by relating opportunity ratings and close dates to a more objective standard of work done (for example, needs analysis completed) and progress made (contact with three senior managers in the buying group) in respect of each account, or opportunity.

- It can reduce reporting time by up to 50%, eliminating manually-compiled call-sheets, spreadsheets, requests for updates, etc. With a sales system implemented consistently, all the information required by managers should be available through dashboards, or easily accessible reports.

- It enables a more sales-led approach to marketing, facilitating a switch from expensive mass marketing (for example, advertising and events) to more measurable direct, or one-to-one, contact with target customers, thus aligning sales and marketing more closely. Other benefits to marketing include the automation of tasks such as capturing web-generated leads, mailing of electronic newsletters, tracking of opt-outs, etc.

- It makes people more productive and efficient, reducing time spent on paperwork, information search, personal organisation (for example, route planning and time management), meeting preparation, and, of course, reporting.

- It maximises collaboration across sales teams, and between sales and marketing, by ensuring access to shared information and tracking of requests / activities / cases across the team.

- It enables managers to track and manage levels of sales activity and effectiveness across the sales cycle, by providing key metrics and KPIs, including number of leads generated, number of sales meetings, or conversion rates at different stages – for example, from lead to meeting, or from cycle to close.

- It makes leading and managing a sales force easier:
  - Since managers have all the information (result of meetings, status with opportunities, etc.) from the system, sales meetings can focus on a transfer of enthusiasm, knowledge and insights, rather than a roll-call of opportunities.
  - Managers get to do more coaching, since the system identifies which sales people, markets or products may be struggling.
  - What gets measured gets done, thus a system generally results in an increase in the levels of sales activity (initially, at least).
  - As sales people are motivated by their performance relative to their peers, the introduction of a system that provides greater visibility of comparative performance, when handled correctly, can spur individual sales people to 'up their game'.

- More and better information is available to the people who need it. Such improved openness and communication generally enhances levels of trust and respect and, in turn, performance. It also enables managers and their people to make better decisions – for example, where to focus limited sales resources, what areas will deliver greatest results, etc. In so many organisations, second-guessing by managers of the activities and progress of salespeople occurs because they do not have accurate information available – this is unhelpful and can be demotivating. A sales system ensures that a sales person and his or her manager are constantly on the same page. It results in clarity of expectations and reduces the likelihood of surprises.

- It allows for proper customer relationship management. Sales databases began as a central repository for customer information and, as their functionality expanded, they became effective tools for managing customer relationships. This is still a vital role for any sales database to perform, enabling managers and their teams to engage in more co-ordinated, systematic and proactive customer contact, resulting in more effective account management, increased customer loyalty and growing customer revenues.

See also

Q94   How do we know our sales system is working properly?
Q95   How do we make our sales system more effective?
Q96   How can we measure user skills on our sales system?
Q97   What can we do when sales staff won't use our sales system?

Q94 How do we know our sales system is working properly?

An essential ingredient of effective sales and marketing in all companies is an up-to-date and easy-to-use database. It drives the sales process – from sales prospecting to account management – making the contribution of all those in sales and marketing focused, efficient and clear.

Here is a checklist to help you examine how effectively your company is using its most important sales and marketing tool:

1. How widely used is the database?

- Do the user logs show regular use by key people?
- How up-to-date is the information?
- How thoroughly used is it (for example, for prospecting, nurturing, tasks completed, etc.)?
- Do key accounts have next actions assigned to various people, with dates for completion of these actions?
- Do all priority accounts have an owner?

2. How easy to use is the database?

- Have users received training?
- Is good documentation available?
- Is support available? Has it been taken advantage of?
- Are key features being used?
- Is there a consistent approach to how information is updated across all users?

3. How much information does it contain?

- Number of accounts (clients, past clients, prospects, etc.), opportunities, contacts and leads?
- By sector / market?

- How representative are accounts of your company's ideal customer-base / target market and its sales and marketing activity for this year?

4. How up-to-date is the information?

- How recent are the last modified dates on key accounts, last dates on actions, cases, etc?
- Is contact information on the accounts and contacts up-to-date?
- How much screening / cleansing of the data is undertaken – and how often / regularly?

5. How thorough / detailed is the information?

- How well kept are records – for example, are there web and address details, company description, contact information, notes of actions / meetings, accurate ratings, etc.?

6. How does the database comply with best practice and the law?

- Does it comply with any legal requirements re direct and database marketing (for example, the Telephone Preference Service (TPS) in the UK)?
- Are opt-outs offered on all emails sent?
- Does your company have a privacy policy (and is it on emails, web sign-ups, etc.)?

7. How well it is managed?

- Does one person have responsibility for it?
- Who is responsible for keeping the information clean and up-to-date?
- Is administrative support available for users in such time-consuming tasks as finding telephone numbers, entering new companies, mail-shots, etc?
- When was the last time there was a discussion on how the database was to be used, or developed?
- Are campaigns run from the database measured for their effectiveness?

- How customised is the database to your company's needs? Are there redundant fields? Are there important fields missing? Have drop-down menus been customised?

8. How effectively does it guide sales activity?

- Can the company's present sales and marketing targets be readily identified from the database?
- Is it used as part of sales campaigns?
- Does it have up-to-date opportunity / forecast information?
- Are top-ranked accounts easy to find and do they have next actions allocated to them?
- Can the activity level of sales people be seen from the database?
- Is it used to trigger next actions in respect of advancing sales cycles, progressing opportunities, nurturing prospects, etc.?

9. How effectively is it employed?

- As a marketing tool (mail-outs, email campaigns, etc.)?
- In monitoring and reporting on the success of campaigns, reporting on activity, etc.?
- As a sales pipeline forecasting and management tool?
- For customer relationship management, fulfilment and other purposes?
- In integrating with other systems (for example, accounting systems)?

10. How effectively is it used in account management?

- Are customer accounts prioritised or categorised in the database?
- Does it have details of account revenue targets and plans?
- Does it record notes of meetings, cases, etc.?
- Does each account have an owner?
- Are the names of all decision-makers and influencers in the account company identified?

- Is there a list of tasks completed and next actions in respect of managing and servicing the account?

11. How does the database perform in terms of:

- Accessibility?
- Security?
- Back-ups?
- Availability (for example, down-time, remote access, etc.)?
- Service / support?
- Integrating with email, document storage, calendar, etc.?
- Reporting functions?
- Customisation available (for example, customisable drop-down menus, etc.)

12. Cost and payback

- What is the annual cost of the system, including licence costs and software (if used), together with time spent gathering and updating information, undertaking mail-outs, set-up and customisation, etc.?
- What is potential value of this information?
- What would the cost be if purchased, or gathered, in other ways?
- Does it save people time, or make them more efficient?

See also

Q95 How do we make our sales system more effective?

Here are nine things you can do to can transform your sales database or CRM system into a powerful sales and marketing tool:

- Purge your database! A database with 200 well-used entries can be much better than a database with 4,000 names that is disorganised and out-of-date. So screen all those contacts, accounts and opportunities in your database, re-classifying them as appropriate (based on relevance and potential). Do a spotcheck on 20 or so entries to see where contact information is out-of-date, or when the last contact is dated; this will help you to set criteria for cleansing the database – for example, identify those past customers who have not purchased in the past year and mark them as priority; eliminate those that have been dormant for more than five years, and so on. Then allocate priority contacts to an owner and assign an action or next step to each of them.

- If it's not working, scrap it: If your existing database is difficult to use, cannot be accessed remotely and does not provide basic functionality, such as diarying next actions, sending emails, capturing web enquiries directly, or providing real-time management reports, then scrap it. From as little as €9 per user per month you can provide your sales team with access to the most sophisticated customer relationship management (CRM) and sales force automation / administration system (SFA). Take out a demo account on Appshore.net, Salesforce.com, Sugar CRM or Sage CRM to see what your sales database can – and should – be.

- Use it for pipeline management and forecasting: Transform your sales database into a powerful management tool, by using it to track leads all the way through to orders. That begins with leads and enquiries, the meetings, opportunities, and deals won. Track progress at each stage, generating metrics to enable you to identify salespeople who may be under-performing, or areas of the sales process that require attention.

- Organise training: Among the key barriers to the more widespread, expert and consistent use of a sales database are the level of skill of, and support available to, users. So classify users into basic, intermediate and advanced user skills, in terms of their present skills levels and what their jobs require. Then organise a programme of training, supported by the necessary manuals, or documentation. Certification may be important to encourage extra effort and commitment.

- Use a common sales process and sales language: Getting the most out of your sales system depends on having a consistent definition of the sales process and sales language across your sales team. That means ensuring the way sales opportunities are ranked is consistent, with the associated probability of closing relating to some agreed and (hopefully) objective standard, in order to curb the natural optimism of the salesperson. Defining your organisation's sales process takes forecasting another step further. For example, if a deal is forecast for January and given a 90% probability, the sales manager can assess the validity of this assessment by reviewing whether key aspects of the sales process have been satisfactorily completed, such as:
  - Identifying and covering the buying group.
  - Formal needs analysis completed.
  - Notes of meeting in the database.
  - Client feedback on draft proposal, etc.

- Put it in people's job descriptions: Encourage people to use the sales database, providing them with the training and support required. But do not stop there. Make its use mandatory. Write the requirement to use the system into job descriptions and job reviews. Calculate commissions and other payments based on sales data as presented in the system.

- Stop relying on spreadsheets: Make your sales database do the work of managing sales opportunities and forecasting sales revenues. This is a real test of the degree to which you are using your system. If your team is putting in the right information and keeping it up-to-date, you should be able to view an up-to-date dashboard of sales KPIs every time you log in.

- Put somebody in charge of it: Give one person overall responsibility for managing the sales database, which includes organisation of the training, reviewing data quality, cleaning out the system, tracking usage levels, managing compliance, etc.

- Run campaigns using it: If you are having problems getting adoption of your sales database, then put some new leads into it and use them to run a campaign. Allocate the leads to various salespeople and direct them to the system to find them. Use the system to send a campaign email, as well as to capture automatically any enquiries made from your website.

See also

Q96 How can we measure user skills on our sales system?

Today's customer relationship management (CRM) and sales force automation / administration (SFA) systems offer impressive functionality, but require higher levels of skill on the part of users. Insufficient, or inadequate, training of users translates into low levels of usage, sales productivity and sales effectiveness.

So, how many of your users are at advanced, expert, or just foundation level? What level do they need to be at, given their various roles? The following checklist will help you to assess the CRM / SFA skills levels of your team and to plan user training.

For each person on your team, put a tick beside the activities they are able to complete. Un-ticked activities represent an ideal starting point for further training.

Level 1: Foundation skills: These are the key tasks, or foundation skills, you need to use a CRM / sales automation tool successfully:

- Can you create an account and set Type, Source, Industry and Rating as appropriate, or to default?
- Can you create a contact in a specific account, add notes of a conversation to it, schedule a call with the contact and send an email to the contact person?
- Can you change your password?
- Can you search for a company or a person in the database and view their information?
- Can you edit a contact and an account and save the changes?
- Can you order accounts in alphabetical order, both in ascending and descending order?
- Can you order accounts by a specific category in rating, type, or source to show only a list of the ones in the category you have chosen? Can you see the number in the category without counting them?

- Can you enlarge the number of accounts shown at any one time to 50?
- Can you send an email with an attachment to yourself and check that it arrives correctly? Can you view the sent email in your sent folder?

Level 2: Advanced skills: Here are the key tasks, or advanced skills, that will demonstrate your proficiency in the use of a CRM / sales automation tool:

- Can you create opportunity, setting probability, start and end dates, etc., and assign a follow-up call to it?
- Can you view an opportunity created in the Forecast tab, viewing it under quarter and year tabs?
- Can you assign an account to another user, view accounts and contacts owner by other users?
- Can you open accounts, or contacts, in edit and in view mode?
- Can you change the dashboard layout? Can you put neglected accounts in the right panel, top activities by priority and by date in the centre column and open cases in the right panel of the screen?
- Can you send a test email using a template and change it if required?
- Can you export a file containing account details for backup?
- Can you upload a document to the database and rename it?

Level 3: Expert user: If you can complete the following tasks, then you have reached an expert level of proficiency in using a CRM / sales management tool, and managing or administrating the system for your company:

- Can you import a list of companies or contacts from an Excel spreadsheet, then set rating, type, source and industry as appropriate to the records entered *en masse*?
- Can you review a selection of six accounts (randomly chosen) in the database? Are they completed correctly? Is each one assigned, is there a next action, is there a type, rating, source and industry

rating? Are notes kept of meetings and conversations? Are emails and documents present?

- Can you quantify and compare activity and progress by two users, in terms of number of accounts / contacts, level of activity and effectiveness?
- Can you generate a report?
- Can you create an email template, using different typefaces and colours? Can you send a test email using the template and make changes as required?
- Can you add a category to the 'type' drop-down menu? Can you then update an account – changing type to the new category you have added?
- Can you add a new user, reset a user password, reset roles, or privileges, change the order in which different applications (accounts, contacts, etc.) are displayed?
- Can you customise the database to company standards: dashboard, drop-down menus, user set-up, etc.?

See also

Q97 What can we do when sales staff won't use our sales system?

Most companies have implemented some form of sales system. However, few have achieved the promised payback on their investment. One of the key reasons is patchy use; our experience shows that such systems are under-used, or not used at all, by a majority of salespeople, sales support and sales administration staff.

Our clients point to seven reasons why people don't use (or don't use properly) their sales systems.

Reason #1: The wrong system has been implemented / inherited – the system in place does not meet user needs. Typically, that means it is:

- Cumbersome, unsteady / unreliable, or slow.
- Difficult to use (rather than being intuitive and easy-to-follow).
- Inadequate in terms of help / instructions.
- Lacking in key functionality (for example, does not have a diary function, or does not allow you to enter 8-digit product codes).
- Not integrated with other applications that staff must already use (resulting in duplication of effort).
- Not tailored to the needs of users (for example, drop-down menus, field names, etc. do not match the business' terms).
- *What to do about it:* Review whether the existing system can be improved, or should be replaced.

Reason #2: The information contained in the system is of poor value – the company and contact information in the system is incomplete, out-of-date, or not relevant. The system is not purged, or updated regularly.

- *What to do about it:* Institute periodic reviews of the quality of the information in the database. Ensure the administrative resource purges the data, replacing redundant information with new target lists and contact information, and importing information kept elsewhere (spreadsheets, Outlook address books, etc.).

Reason #3: The system has been implemented without sufficient user buy-in, or understanding of the benefits (both to users and to the company overall).

- *What to do about it:* Re-launch the system, starting with one small group of users who can benefit immediately from using the system (or are suffering as a result of not being able to use it) and provide the support to enable them to reap the benefits for themselves. With this group as advocates, spread news of the benefits to others.

Reason #4: A lack of leadership – the system is not being used, or aggressively promoted, by sales managers or directors.

- *What to do about it:* If the sales manager does not use the sales database, then he / she is not in a position to expect anything different from others. He / she must demonstrate a commitment / competency in respect of using the system. That includes moving from spreadsheet-based forecasting and paper-based sales reports, to conducting every conversation with reps or the team by reviewing the relevant account, opportunity or lead in the database only.

Reason #5: Lack of appropriate incentives, where the proper usage of the system is not written into job descriptions, staff and team performance reviews, or linked into the receipt of bonus and commission payments.

- *What to do about it:* Job descriptions should stipulate that keeping sales records, account and contact information up-to-date in the sales system (including notes of meetings, telephone conversation, etc.) is essential. This aspect of job-related performance should be reviewed formally at staff reviews and linked to payments of bonuses or commissions.

Reason #6: Inadequate system administration and support to users, including help in terms of lost passwords, user problems, importing lists, organising mail-outs, etc.

- *What to do about it:* Every database or CRM system requires an administrator. But that is not just somebody who can, when requested, set up a user, or change a password. There is a more active role of reviewing usage levels on an ongoing basis to ensure users have the skills required, that data is being entered in the correct / uniform manner, that neglected leads, accounts, or opportunities are being followed up, etc. It is also a resource that can pro-actively anticipate and meet the needs of users and teams, such as assisting in the creation of new lists for entry to the database, input of sales letters, proposal and other templates, etc. – all designed to ensure that users can gain the maximum benefit from the system.

Reason #7: Insufficient, or inadequate training of users. That means not just an intensive one-day training session, but periodic training towards a progressive building of skills, from foundation to expert levels (depending on the specific role and requirements of the user).

- *What to do about it:* Today's customer relationship management and sales force automation / administration (SFA) systems offer impressive functionality, but require higher levels of skill on the part of users. Although salespeople may have little time, or patience, for office-based training, or indeed may not even admit that it is needed, one of the key reasons why sales systems are not used is the frustration experienced by users who have inadequate systems familiarity, or skills. Training participation must be mandatory, with certification and subsequent access to ongoing training and intensive support, based on scheduled follow-ups between each salesperson and the system administrator.

See also

Q98 How can we improve our recruitment of sales staff?

The success rate for new sales hires is a miserable 33% - at best. That means adding a new salesperson to your team is one of the riskiest gambles you can take. Given recruitment fees and long lead-in times, it is also one of the most expensive.

Picking sales and marketing people is more difficult than picking any other candidates. With that in mind, here are the top five mistakes made in their recruitment:

- Job description too broad – essentially combining two or more specific roles into the one or too vague – for example, make and log telephone calls with a minimum of X potential customers per week.

- Not asking practical questions – for example, "We are beginning a marketing drive in the UK in May, if you had responsibility for it what specifically would you do ensure its success? What would be your focus in week 1 of the job?", etc.

- Not asking sufficiently detailed questions about previous roles, activities and achievements and then following up on references.

- Not getting off to a good start – the first month or two are a golden period; if it is not successful and the candidate is not managed properly in this period, it is very difficult to change later.

- Failing to ensure the candidate is a hard worker, with an action-bias and practical bent. As somebody once said "'I would rather have a body without a suit, than a suit without a body".

See also

Q90 Who do we need on our selling team?

Q99   What should our sales plan look like?

No manager wants to spend days writing a sales plan, and no rep, manager, or investor wants to spend hours reading such a plan either. Everybody agrees that a plan is required, but how to keep it short and at the same include all those key elements that will ensure the sales team stays on course for the year?

Here are some of the key ingredients included in the best sales plans:

- Too many sales drives stumble at the first hurdle, that is, lead generation. So your plan must include a target and budget for lead generation from multiple sources over time.

- Activity gets results and, for many managers, getting the level of sales activity up (for example, getting in front of more prospects) is a key priority. However, targets and plans in this area must be balanced with the need to improve sales effectiveness. Quite simply, it is better to do 10 meetings and convert 20%, than to do 20 meetings and convert just 10%.

- Too many plans are short on specifics, in particular metrics and KPIs that can be used to track progress on a weekly, or monthly basis, including number of meetings, conversion rate from lead to meeting, from proposals to orders, etc.

- Set a target for new and existing revenues, and set a target for up-selling and cross-selling. Outline targets for growing revenue in key accounts and key account management and customer service priorities / policies.

- Focus on a number of campaigns, around which you can centre your activities. Don't have one plan for marketing and another for sales, but a consistent and integrated campaign arranged on a quarterly basis, for example. Agree the message for each, the target list / target list profile for each, etc.

- Help individual sales people put together a two-page plan for themselves. Nobody is more committed to a plan than if they write it themselves. In addition, this an ideal opportunity to coach them towards achieving their full potential. Your overall sales plan is the summation of all the individual sales plans of your team.

- Don't beat around the bush. State exactly how many leads and meetings will be required for each sales person per week, or per month in order to achieve target.

- In your overall plan, focus on this / next quarter in detail, relating it to the individual sales plans of each of the sales people and the overall campaign set out. Include a rigorous validation of the pipeline, related to the key stages of your sales process.

- Focus on the issues of sales process, sales systems, sales structures, etc., identifying opportunities to ensure the smooth running of your sales organisation / sales team.

See also

Q13   What are the six challenges lead generation must overcome?
Q92   How can we be better at sales forecasting?
Q100   How can we increase the effectiveness of our sales team?

QUICK WIN MARKETING Q15 What's in a sales plan?
QUICK WIN MARKETING Q71 How do we manage a sales plan to ensure that we achieve our targets?

Q100   How can we increase the effectiveness of our sales team?

Here are 10 things you can do as a sales manager to improve the sales performance of your team:

- Run a sales campaign (providing the impetus of specific sales campaigns supported by marketing initiatives).
- Implement a sales system (making target lists, sales planning, reporting and administration, as well as marketing much more efficient and allowing metrics regarding activity and effectiveness to be easily tracked across the sales team).
- Revise your sales process (pre-qualification, more systematic needs analysis, relationship building, etc.).
- Improve your sales structures (including incentives, meetings, reviews, etc.).
- Provide better leadership and more coaching in the field.
- Provide sales / marketing / telesales support (including list-building, generating awareness / enquiries, appointment setting, etc.).
- Provide sales training – building confidence and skill, as well as product and industry knowledge.
- Segment your market (targeting specific niches or segments in a tailored and effective manner).
- Revise your sales materials / collateral (updating tired sales aids, brochures, web pages, etc.).
- Revisit your sales proposition (putting a new, more compelling angle on the message for the customer).

ABOUT THE AUTHORS

John and Ray are successful salespeople turned sales consultants. They come at selling from a new angle — that of the buyer.

Ray Collis has consulted to companies such as Smith&Nephew, Nilfisk, BT Wholesale and Norsk Hydro. He has Master's and Bachelor's degrees in Business and Marketing.

John O'Gorman has sold and consulted internationally for organisations such as Digital, Compaq and Eontec (acquired by Siebel). He completed his International MBA in 2004 and holds a Bachelor of Commerce degree.

John and Ray act as sales advisors to ambitious sales organisations, government agencies and educational institutions. Visit their web portal, **www.sellerinsights.com**, for 1000s of insights, tips and techniques.

ABOUT THE QUICK WIN SERIES

The **Quick Win** series of books, apps and websites is designed for the modern, busy reader, who wants to learn enough to complete the immediate task at hand, but needs to see the information in context.

Topics published to date include:

- QUICK WIN MARKETING.
- QUICK WIN DIGITAL MARKETING.

Topics planned for 2010 include:

- QUICK WIN ECONOMICS.
- QUICK WIN MEDIA LAW IRELAND.
- QUICK WIN LEADERSHIP.
- QUICK WIN LEAN BUSINESS.
- QUICK WIN SAFETY MANAGEMENT.
- QUICK WIN SMALL BUSINESS.

For more information, see **www.oaktreepress.com**.

Lightning Source UK Ltd.
Milton Keynes UK
29 September 2010

160555UK00001B/7/P

9 781904 887485